GAS ENGINE CONSTRUCTION AND OPERATION

NATEF Standards Lab Manual—AT 101

Jack Erjavec/Jim Clarke

Vice President, Technology and Trades SBU:
Alar Elken

Editorial Director:
Sandy Clark

Senior Acquisitions Editor:
David Boelio

Development Editor:
Christopher Shortt

Marketing Director:
Dave Garza

Channel Manager:
Bill Lawrensen

Marketing Coordinator:
Mark Pierro

Production Director:
Mary Ellen Black

Production Manager:
Larry Main

Production Coordinator:
Dawn Jacobson

Project Editor:
Toni Hansen

Art-Design Specialist
Rachel Baker

Editorial Assistant:
Kevin Rivenburg

COPYRIGHT © 2005 Thomson Delmar Learning. Thomson, the Star Logo, and Delmar Learning are trademarks used herein under license.

Printed in Canada
6 XX 06

For more information contact
Thomson Delmar Learning
Executive Woods
5 Maxwell Drive, PO Box 8007,
Clifton Park, NY 12065-8007
Or find us on the World Wide Web at
www.delmarlearning.com

ALL RIGHTS RESERVED. No part of this work covered by the copyright hereon may be reproduced in any form or by any means—graphic, electronic, or mechanical, including photocopying, recording, taping, Web distribution, or information storage and retrieval systems—without the written permission of the publisher.

For permission to use material from the text or product, contact us by
Tel.   (800) 730-2214
Fax   (800) 730-2215
www.thomsonrights.com

Library of Congress Cataloging-in-Publication Data:
Card Number:

ISBN: 1-4018-8111-4

NOTICE TO THE READER

Publisher does not warrant or guarantee any of the products described herein or perform any independent analysis in connection with any of the product information contained herein. Publisher does not assume, and expressly disclaims, any obligation to obtain and include information other than that provided to it by the manufacturer.

The reader is expressly warned to consider and adopt all safety precautions that might be indicated by the activities herein and to avoid all potential hazards. By following the instructions contained herein, the reader willingly assumes all risks in connection with such instructions.

The publisher makes no representation or warranties of any kind, including but not limited to, the warranties of fitness for particular purpose or merchantability, nor are any such representations implied with respect to the material set forth herein, and the publisher takes no responsibility with respect to such material. The publisher shall not be liable for any special, consequential, or exemplary damages resulting, in whole or part, from the readers' use of, or reliance upon, this material.

CONTENTS

Introduction Information Sheet	1

CHAPTER 8 Automotive Engine Design and Diagnostics

Information Sheet/Automotive Engine Design and Diagnostics	3
Job Sheet AT 101-1/ Introduction to AT 101	5
Job Sheet AT 101-2/ Safety and Accident Prevention (Ch. 3)	7
Job Sheet AT 101-3/ Verifying the Condition and Inspecting an Engine (Ch. 8)	11
Job Sheet AT 101-4/ Engine Identification (Ch. 5)	19
Shop Activity AT 101-1 (Ch. 8)	23
Shop Activity AT 101-2 (Ch. 8)	25
Review Questions	27

CHAPTER 9 Engine Disassembly

Information Sheet/Engine Disassembly	29
Job Sheet AT 101-5/ Remove and Disassemble Cylinder Head (Ch. 9)	31
Job Sheet AT 101-6/ Remove Cylinder Ring Ridge (Ch. 9)	35
Shop Activity AT 101-3 (Ch. 9)	37
Shop Activity AT 101-4 (Ch. 9)	41
Case Study (Ch. 9)	42
Review Questions	43

CHAPTER 10 Short Blocks

Information Sheet/Short Blocks	45
Job Sheet AT 101-7/ Engine Block Inspection (Ch. 8)	47
Job Sheet AT 101-8/ Deglaze and Clean Cylinder Walls (Ch. 8)	51
Job Sheet AT 101-9/ Measure Cylinder Bore (Ch. 10)	53
Job Sheet AT 101-10/ Measure Crankshaft Bearing Journals (Ch. 10)	57
Job Sheet AT 101-11/ Measure Camshaft Lobes/Bearing Journals (Ch. 10)	61
Job Sheet AT 101-12/ Install Camshaft Bearings (Ch. 10)	65
Job Sheet AT 101-13/ Inspect and Replace Camshaft Drives (Ch. 10)	69
Job Sheet AT 101-14/ Test for Worn Cam Lobes (Ch. 10)	71
Job Sheet AT 101-15/ Checking and Servicing Pistons and Pins (Ch. 8)	75
Job Sheet AT 101-16/ Install Pistons and Connecting Rods (Ch. 10)	79
Shop Activity AT 101-5 (Ch. 10)	81
Shop Activity AT 101-6 (Ch. 10)	83
Shop Activity AT 101-7 (Ch. 10)	85
Shop Activity AT 101-8 (Ch. 10)	87
Shop Activity AT 101-9 (Ch. 10)	89
Review Questions	91

CHAPTER 11 Cylinder Heads and Valves

Information Sheet/Cylinder Heads and Valves	95
Job Sheet AT 101-17/ Inspect Cylinder Head for Wear (Ch. 11)	97
Job Sheet AT 101-18/ Inspect and Test Valve Springs for Squareness, Pressure, and Free Height Comparison (Ch. 11)	103
Job Sheet AT 101-19/ Inspecting Valve Spring Retainers, Locks, and Valve Lock Grooves (Ch. 11)	105
Job Sheet AT 101-20/ Recondition Valve Faces (Ch. 11)	107
Case Study (Ch. 11)	109
Job Sheet AT 101-21/ Inspect Valve Lifters, Pushrods, and Rocker Arms (Ch. 11)	111
Job Sheet AT 101-22/ Valve Seat Reconditioning (Ch. 11)	113
Job Sheet AT 101-23/ Install Cylinder Heads and Gaskets (Ch. 10)	117
Job Sheet AT 101-24/ Valve Timing Check (Ch. 11)	119
Job Sheet AT 101-25/ Replace a Timing Belt on an OHC Engine (Ch. 11)	121
Job Sheet AT 101-26/ Servicing Oil Pressure and Temperature Sensors (Ch. 11 & Ch. 20)	125
Shop Activity AT 101-10 (Ch. 11)	129
Shop Activity AT 101-11 (Ch. 11)	133
Case Study (Ch. 11)	134
Review Questions	135

CHAPTER 13 Engine Sealing and Reassembly

Information Sheet/Engine Sealing and Reassembly	137
Job Sheet AT 101-27/ Reassemble Engine (Ch. 13)	139
Job Sheet AT 101-28/ Adjust Valves on an OHC Engine (Ch.11)	143
Job Sheet AT 101-29/ Applying RTV Silicone Sealant (Ch. 13)	145
Job Sheet AT 101-30/ Prime an Engine's Lubrication System (Ch. 13)	147
Shop Activity AT 101-12 (Ch. 4)	149
Shop Activity AT 101-13 (Ch. 13)	151
Review Questions	153
ASE Prep Test	154

INTRODUCTION INFORMATION SHEET

AT 101 / GAS ENGINES

A vehicle's engine is a complex piece of precision-built machinery. You must have a clear understanding of how the internal combustion process of an engine generates usable power before you attempt any engine work.

Engine repair and rebuilding procedures are among the most demanding jobs performed by the service technician. Components must be handled with great care and be assembled to exacting tolerances. Absolute cleanliness must be maintained. Bolt torque and sealing requirements must be met.

Most of the shop activities in this section are aimed at familiarizing the student with the various aspects of engine rebuilding. Diagnostic charts provide guidance in troubleshooting the lubrication and cooling systems. The job sheets acquaint the student with many of the engine repair and rebuilding procedures covered by the ASE Engine Repair Test. Case studies will encourage and strengthen the student's skill in the use of service manuals and logical diagnostic skills.

INFORMATION SHEET

Automotive Engine Design and Diagnostics

INFORMATION

These job sheets cover the fundamentals of engine operation: the four-stroke cycle and the major components. They also cover common tests conducted to diagnose engine problems. These tests should be conducted whenever an engine mechanical problem is suspected.

The engine provides the power to drive a vehicle's wheels. All automobile engines are classified as internal combustion engines because the combustion process (or burning of the fuel) takes place inside the engine, this is true for diesel and gasoline internal combustion engines.

The biggest part of the engine is the cylinder block. The cylinder block is a large metal casting that is drilled to allow for the passage of lubricants and coolant to flow through it. It is also drilled to allow the various moving parts the space needed to operate within it. The block contains round passages, which are called cylinders. These cylinders contain pistons, which are specially-machined pieces of aluminum alloy material designed to operate under extreme temperature and pressure conditions.

The cylinder head fits on top of the cylinder block to close off and seal the top of the cylinder to create the combustion chamber. The combustion chamber is the area where the air/fuel mixture is compressed and burned. The cylinder head also contains ports through which the air/fuel mixture enters the combustion chamber and the burned gases exit.

The valve train is a series of parts used to open and close the intake and exhaust ports. A valve is a movable part that opens and closes the ports. A camshaft controls the movement of the valves. Springs are used to help close the valves.

The up and down motion of the pistons must be converted to a rotary motion before it can drive the wheels of the vehicle. This conversion is achieved by linking the piston to a crankshaft with a connecting rod. The upper end of the connecting rod moves with the piston. The lower end of the connecting rod is attached to the crankshaft and moves in a circle. The end of the crankshaft is connected to the flywheel.

Nearly all automotive engines run through a four-stroke cycle in order to produce power. These strokes repeat themselves, in each cylinder, several times per minute. The name of the stroke defines what is taking place during its cycle. There is an intake stroke during which the atomized air/fuel mixture is pushed into the combustion chamber. The compression stroke compresses the air/fuel mixture. The power stroke is when the compressed air/fuel mixture is ignited, driving the piston downward in the cylinder. The exhaust stroke is when the burned gases from the power stroke are pushed out of the combustion chamber.

☐ JOB SHEET / AT 101-1

Introduction to AT 101

Name _____ Station _____ Date _____

Objective

Upon completion of this job sheet, you will be able to state the objectives of this course, the general rules of attendance, use of equipment and facilities, and the standards of performance expected for this course.

Tools and Materials:
Instructor-provided references
Student handbook
AUTOMOTIVE TECHNOLOGY 4e (Thomson, Delmar Learning)

Protective Gear:
N/A

Describe the vehicle being worked on:
Year _____ Make _____ Model _____
VIN _____ Engine type and size _____

PROCEDURE

Answer the following questions in your own words. Answers will be discussed in class. Any questions you may have can be addressed during the discussion period.

A. Did you receive a copy of the school catalog? _____

B. Did you receive a copy of the student handbook? _____

C. Have you read the handbook and catalog? _____

D. What is the required attendance percentage to complete this course? _____

E. What is the minimum grade to pass this class? _____

F. What is the minimum required Grade Point Average required to graduate? _____

G. List five service operations you expect to be able to perform after taking this course.

   1. _____
   2. _____
   3. _____
   4. _____
   5. _____

H. List four items you must bring to class every day.

   1._____

   2._____

   3._____

   4._____

I. Who is responsible for the cleanliness of your work area? _____

J. Assume you are sick on Monday and Tuesday, and you are not sure if you will be able to attend class the rest of the week. What should you do?

   _____

K. Write down any questions you may have, and bring them up during the discussion portion of this lesson.

   _____

   _____

   _____

L. Reading Assignments   Page Number   Source

   1. _____   _____   _____

   2. _____   _____   _____

   3. _____   _____   _____

   4. _____   _____   _____

   5. _____   _____   _____

   6. _____   _____   _____

   7. _____   _____   _____

   8. _____   _____   _____

   9. _____   _____   _____

   10. _____   _____   _____

M. List the proper procedures to follow to bring a vehicle into the school's shop.

   _____

   _____

Problems Encountered

_____

_____

_____

Instructor's Comments

_____

_____

_____

☐ JOB SHEET AT / 101-2

Safety and Accident Prevention

Name _____ Station _____ Date _____

Objective

Upon completion of this job sheet, you will gain the understanding of the importance of safety, accident, and fire prevention.

Refer to **Chapter 3** in the AUTOMOTIVE TECHNOLOGY book for additional information.

These job sheets meet the requirements for **NATEF** task(s): **Engine Repair**

Tools and Materials:
AUTOMOTIVE TECHNOLOGY 4e (Thomson, Delmar Learning)
Instructor Notes
LTI Handbook

Protective Gear:
N/A

Describe the vehicle being worked on:
Year _____ Make _____ Model _____
VIN _____ Engine type and size _____

PROCEDURE

Select the best answers for the following questions:

1. What is the first task to perform in case an accident has occurred?

    a. Notify your instructor immediately.

    b. Call the police.

    c. Send for the school nurse.

    d. Treat yourself when you exit the school.

2. Technician A says that carbon monoxide from a vehicle exhaust can kill you.
   Technician B says you can smell carbon monoxide and should be aware of the sweet odor.
   Who is correct?

    a. Technician A

    b. Technician B

    c. Both A and B

    d. Neither A nor B

3. Electric cooling fans used on some automobiles:

    a. Are dangerous and should always be disconnected when servicing components near them.

    b. Are unpredictable and can start up at any time possibly causing personal injury.

    c. Both a and b are correct and should be remembered at all times.

    d. Is not a concern to the technician working under the hood.

4. If battery acid gets into your eyes, you should immediately:

    a. Flush your eyes with water and notify your instructor.

    b. Put your safety goggles on.

    c. Keep your eyes closed.

    d. Rub your eyes until they water.

5. An electrical fire is a class C fire. What type of fire extinguisher should you use on a class C fire?

    a. Water

    b. Carbon dioxide

    c. Dry Chemical

    d. Either a or c

6. What is the first thing you should do if you see a fire?

    a. Report it to your instructor

    b. Activate the fire alarm.

    c. Evacuate the area.

    d. Tell another student.

7. The negative battery cable on an automobile should be disconnected:

    a. First.

    b. Last.

    c. It makes no difference one way or the other.

    d. None of the above.

8. What should a technician do to prevent an electrostatic discharge from damaging sensitive electronic components?

    a. Avoid touching the electrical terminals.

    b Always touch a known good ground before handling an electrical component.

    c. Wear a grounding strap.

    d. Both a and b are acceptable methods.

9. Ringing in the ears and headaches can be signs of:

    a. Carbon monoxide poisoning.

    b. Too much noise in the shop.

    c. Too much oxygen.

    d. None of the above.

10. Which of the following rules should be followed when moving a vehicle into or around the shop?

    a. Use extreme caution when moving a vehicle; check around the vehicle and the planned path to make sure no obstacles are in the way.

    b. Use a spotter to help move or park a vehicle in a closed area.

    c. Wear your safety belt whenever you are in a moving vehicle no matter how short the ride.

    d. All of the above.

11. Which of the following is the golden rule that applies to each tool, machine, or piece of equipment you may operate during your training at LTI?

    a. Operate equipment only after receiving training on how to use it properly and safely.

    b. Operate equipment only when your instructor is with you.

    c. Operate equipment only after your lab partner has demonstrated how he or she uses it.

    d. Operate equipment at your own risk.

12. Who is financially responsible for tools that are lost or broken due to negligence?

    a. LTI is responsible for all tools it provides.

    b. The student that signs the tool out from his/her instructor or tool person.

    c. The student that last used the tool.

    d. Things just happen, no one is responsible.

Problems Encountered

_____
_____
_____

Instructor's Comments

_____
_____
_____

☐ JOB SHEET / AT 101-3

Verifying the Condition of and Inspecting an Engine

Name _____ Station _____ Date _____

Objective

Upon completion of this job sheet, you will be able to verify and interpret engine concerns; inspect an engine assembly for fuel, oil, coolant, and other leaks; diagnose engine noises and vibrations; and diagnose the cause of oil consumption, unusual engine exhaust color, odor, sounds. You must know how to perform these tasks to pass the ASE Engine Repair and Engine Performance Tests.

Refer to **Chapter 8** in the AUTOMOTIVE TECHNOLOGY book for additional information.

These job sheets meet the requirements for **NATEF** task(s): **General Engine Diagnosis**

Tools and Materials:
AUTOMOTIVE TECHNOLOGY 4e (Thomson, Delmar Learning)
Instructor-designated vehicle
Stethoscope

Protective Gear:
Safety goggles or glasses with side shields

NATEF TASKS
I. Engine Repair
Category: A
Task: 1 (P-1)
Task: 2 (P-1)
Task: 3 (P-1)
Task: 4 (P-1)
Task: 6 (P-2)

Describe the vehicle being worked on:
Year _____ Make _____ Model _____
VIN _____ Engine type and size _____

PROCEDURE: Using instructor-supplied information, answer the following questions.

Verify Engine Condition

1. Verifying the customer's complaint is typically the first step you should take when diagnosing a problem. If the owner of the vehicle stated a concern, describe it. If there are no customer complaints, describe the general running condition to the best of your knowledge. The concern may be one of performance, smoke, leaks, or noises. In your answer, be sure to completely describe the condition and where, when, and how the condition could occur.

_____
_____
_____
_____

2. Verify the complaint. Describe what you would do to duplicate the condition. Include in this description conditions that will explain when, where, and how the condition could occur.

___

WARNING: *Gasoline fumes are extremely dangerous! If ignited, they will cause a very serious explosion and fire, resulting in personal injury and property damage. If you suspect a leak to be fuel, immediately inform your instructor of the problem and take all precautions to avoid igniting the fuel.*

3. Engine fuel leaks are dangerous and expensive; they should be corrected immediately when they are detected. If gasoline odor occurs inside or near a vehicle, it should immediately be inspected for possible fuel leakage. Inspect the following parts of the vehicle to locate the source of the fuel leak. Describe what you found at each of these components.

    A. Fuel tank:

    ___

    B. Fuel tank filler cap:

    ___

    C. Fuel lines and filter:

    ___

    D. Mechanical or external fuel pump:

    ___

    E. Vapor recovery system lines:

    ___

    F. Carburetor (if equipped):

    ___

    G. Pressure regulator, fuel rail, and injectors (fuel injected vehicles):

    ___

4. Based on the above inspection, what do you recommend should be done to correct the fuel leak?

    ___

5. Engine oil leaks may cause an engine to run out of oil, resulting in serious engine damage. Sometimes the leak goes unnoticed, and yet the engine's oil needs to be added to more often than normal. A careful inspection may help you locate the source of the leak; however, if it is difficult to locate the exact cause of the leak, the engine should be thoroughly cleaned. Carefully look at the following engine parts and describe what you see. If oil is found in, on, or around any of theses parts, look carefully above the component directly above the leak. Oil runs down engine surfaces. Also, if an oil leak is found, check the PCV system for blockage and proper operation. A malfunctioning PCV system allows excessive crankcase pressure to build causing early failure of seals and gaskets, resulting in engine oil leaks.

A. Rear main oil seal:
_____

B. Expansion plug for the rear camshaft bearing:
_____

C. Rear oil galley plug:
_____

D. Oil pan:
_____

E. Oil filter:
_____

F. Rocker arm covers:
_____

G. Intake manifold front and rear gaskets (on "V" type engines):
_____

H. Mechanical fuel pump gasket or worn fuel pump pivot pin:
_____

I. Timing gear cover or seal:
_____

J. Front main bearing seal:
_____

K. Oil pressure sending unit:
_____

L. Distributor "O" ring gasket:
_____

M. Engine casting for porosity:
_____

N. Oil cooler lines (where applicable):
_____

6. Based on the above inspection, what do you recommend should be done to the vehicle to correct the oil leak(s)?
_____
_____

7. If an engine uses excessive oil and there is no evidence of external leakage, the oil may be burning in the combustion chambers. If excessive amounts of oil are burned in the combustion chambers, the exhaust contains blue smoke, and the spark plugs may be fouled with oil. Worn rings and cylinders or worn valve guides and valve seals may cause excessive oil burning in the combustion chambers. Remove the spark plugs and record the condition of each.

   #1 _____

   #2 _____

   #3 _____

   #4 _____

   #5 _____

   #6 _____

   #7 _____

   #8 _____

8. When an engine coolant leak causes low coolant level, the engine quickly overheats and severe engine damage may occur. When you suspect a coolant leak, check the following components and describe your findings below.

   A. Upper radiator hose:

   B. Lower radiator hose:

   C. Heater hoses:

   D. By-pass hose:

   E. Water pump:

   F. Engine expansion plugs or block heater:

   G. Radiator:

   H. Thermostat housing:

   I. Heater core:

Automotive Engine Design and Diagnostics **15**

9. Some engine coolant leaks are not visible. A whitish exhaust may be indicative of this sort of coolant leak if it is caused by a leaking head gasket or cracked engine components. Take a look at the exhaust while the engine is idling and describe it:

_____

_____

10. A cooling system pressure tester is commonly used to locate leaks. The use of this tester is covered in another job sheet. What job sheet number and page can this procedure be found on?

Engine Exhaust Diagnosis

1. Some engine problems may be diagnosed by the color, smell, or sound of the exhaust. If the engine is operating normally, the exhaust should be colorless. In severely cold weather, it is normal to see a swirl of white vapor coming from the tailpipe, especially when the engine and exhaust system are cold. This vapor is moisture in the exhaust, which is a normal by-product of the combustion process. Carefully observe the exhaust from your test vehicle and describe what you see and/or smell during the following operating conditions.

   A. Cold start up:

   _____

   B. Cold idle:

   _____

   C. Warm start up:

   _____

   D. Warm idle:

   _____

   E. Snap-throttle open:

   _____

   F. Snap-throttle closed:

   _____

2. Based on the above, what are your conclusions? (Use the explanations below to guide your thoughts.)

   _____

   _____

   - If the exhaust is blue, excessive amounts of oil are entering the combustion chamber, and this oil is being burned with the fuel. When the blue smoke in the exhaust is more noticeable on deceleration, the oil is likely passing the piston rings into the cylinder. If the blue smoke appears in the exhaust immediately after a hot engine is restarted, the oil is likely leaking down the valve guides.
   - If black smoke appears in the exhaust, the air-fuel mixture is too rich. A restriction in the air intake, such as a plugged air filter, may be responsible for a rich air-fuel mixture.
   - Gray smoke in the exhaust may be caused by coolant leaking into the combustion chamber. This may be noticeable when the engine is first started or after it has been shut off for over 30 minutes.

- On catalytic converter-equipped vehicles, a strong sulfur smell in the exhaust indicates a rich air-fuel mixture. Some sulfur smell on these engines is normal, especially during warmup.

3. You may have noticed a change in sound during the above test. If you did, describe the sound change and operating mode in which the sound changed.

_____

_____

_____

_____

4. Use these guidelines to determine the possible cause of the sound. Then state your best guess for the cause of the noise.
   - When the engine is idling, the exhaust at the tailpipe should have a smooth, even sound.
   - If, during idle, the exhaust has a "puff" sound at regular intervals, a cylinder may be misfiring.
   - When this sound is present check the engine's ignition and fuel systems, and the engine's compression.
   - If the vehicle has excessive exhaust noise, while the engine is accelerated, check the exhaust system for leaks.
   - A small exhaust leak may cause a whistling noise when the engine is accelerated.
   - If the exhaust system produces a rattling noise when the engine is accelerated, check the muffler and catalytic converter for loose internal components
   - When the engine has a wheezing noise at idle or with the engine running at higher rpm, check for a restricted exhaust system.

_____

_____

_____

Engine Noise Diagnosis

1. Sound from the engine itself can help you locate engine problems or help you identify a weakness in the engine before it becomes a big problem. Long before a serious engine failure occurs, there are usually warning noises from the engine. Engine defects such as damaged pistons, worn rings, loose piston pins, worn crankshaft bearings, worn camshaft lobes, and loose and worn valve train components usually produce their own peculiar noises. Certain engine defects also cause a noise under specific engine operating conditions. Since it is sometimes difficult to determine the exact location of an engine noise, a stethoscope may be useful. The stethoscope probe is placed on, or near, the suspected component, and the ends of the stethoscope are installed in your ears. The stethoscope amplifies sound to assist in noise location. When the stethoscope probe is moved closer to the source of the noise, the sound is louder in your ears. If a stethoscope is not available, what can be safely used to amplify the sound and help locate the source of the noise? _____

   CAUTION: *When placing a stethoscope probe in various locations on a running engine, be careful not to catch the probe or your hands in moving components such as cooling fan blades and belts.*

Automotive Engine Design and Diagnostics   17

2. Since a lack of lubrication is a common cause of engine noise, always check the engine oil level and condition prior to noise diagnosis. Carefully observe the oil for contamination by coolant or gasoline. Check the oil level and condition on your test vehicle, then record your findings:

_____
_____

3. During the diagnosis of engine noises, always operate the engine under the same conditions as those that are present when the noise ordinarily occurs. Remember that aluminum engine components such as pistons expand more when heated than cast iron alloy components do. Therefore, a noise caused by a piston defect may occur when the engine is cold but disappear when the engine reaches normal operating temperature. If the customer has an engine noise concern, describe the noise and state when it occurs.

_____
_____
_____

4. Duplicate the condition at which the noise typically occurs and describe all that you hear as you listen to the engine.

_____
_____

5. If you verified the customer's concern, use a stethoscope to find the spot where the noise is the loudest. Describe where that is:

_____
_____

6. What could be causing the noise to be loud at that spot?

_____
_____

7. To help you understand and use noise as a diagnostic tool, you will be given a description of an engine noise. Using your knowledge and any resources (such as your text book) you have handy, identify the conditions or problems that would cause each of the following noises:

   A. A hollow, rapping noise that is most noticeable on acceleration with the engine cold. The noise may disappear when the engine reaches normal operating temperature.

   _____

   B. A heavy thumping knock for a brief time when the engine if first started after it has been shut off for several hours. This noise may also be noticeable on hard acceleration.

   _____

   C. A sharp, metallic, rapping noise that occurs with the engine idling.

   _____

   D. A thumping noise at the back of the engine.

   _____

E. A rumbling or thumping noise at the front of the engine, possibly accompanied by engine vibrations. When the engine is accelerated under load, the noise is more noticeable.

F. A light, rapping noise at speeds above 35 mph (21 kph). The noise may vary from a light to a heavier rapping sound depending on the severity of the condition. If the condition is very bad, the noise may be evident when the engine is idling.

G. A high-pitched, clicking noise is noticeable in the upper cylinder area during acceleration.

H. A heavy clicking noise is heard with the engine running at 2,000 to 3,000 rpm. When the condition is severe, a continuous, heavy clicking noise is evident at idle speed.

I. A whirring and light rattling noise when the engine is accelerated and decelerated. Severe cases may cause these noises at idle speed.

J. A light clicking noise with the engine idling. This noise is slower than piston or connecting rod noise and is less noticeable when the engine is accelerated.

K. A high-pitched clicking noise that intensifies when the engine is accelerated.

L. A noise that is similar to marbles rattling inside a metal can. This noise usually occurs when the engine is accelerated.

Problems Encountered

Instructor's Comments

SHOP ACTIVITY / AT 101-2

Engine Identification

Name _____ Station _____ Date _____

Objective

Upon completion of this activity, you will be able to demonstrate how to decipher a VIN code.

Refer to **Chapter 8** in the AUTOMOTIVE TECHNOLOGY book for additional information.

Tools and Materials:
AUTOMOTIVE TECHNOLOGY 4e (Thomson, Delmar Learning)
Instructor Notes
Service Manual

NATEF TASKS
I. Engine Repair
Category: A
Task: 3 (P-1)

Protective Gear:
Safety glasses or goggles as required

Describe the vehicle being worked on:
Year _____ Make _____ Model _____
VIN _____ Engine type and size _____

PROCEDURE

Select a vehicle and write down its VIN code. Using a service manual and the textbook, explain all of the information that is given in the VIN by deciphering the codes.

_____
_____
_____
_____
_____
_____
_____
_____
_____

Problems Encountered

Instructor's Comments

Instructor's Signature

INFORMATION SHEET

Engine Disassembly

INFORMATION

These job sheets cover the basic disassembly procedures required to prepare an engine for a proper rebuild or overhaul.

Disassembling an engine is not just a matter of taking it apart. Always check the service manual for the correct procedure for disassembling the engine you are working on. Failure to follow the correct procedures could result in damage to otherwise reusable components. You should always remove one part at a time, inspect the part, and set it aside. It is wise to keep all removed fasteners with the part they were removed with.

Engine Disassembly   31

☐ **JOB SHEET / AT 101-5**

Remove and Disassemble Cylinder Head

Name _____ Station _____ Date _____

Objective

Upon completion of this job sheet, you will have demonstrated the ability to remove and disassemble a cylinder head properly. You must know how to remove a cylinder head in order to pass the ASE Engine Repair Test. Before beginning, review the sections under the "Cylinder Head Removal" and "Cylinder Head Disassembly" headings in **Chapter 9** of AUTOMOTIVE TECHNOLOGY.

These job sheets meet the requirements for **NATEF** task(s): **Cylinder Head and Valve Train Diagnosis and Repair.**

Tools and Materials:

AUTOMOTIVE TECHNOLOGY 4e (Thomson, Delmar Learning)

Service manual   Soft-faced hammer
Small magnet   Valve spring compressor
Sockets   Valve storage tray

NATEF TASKS
I. Engine Repair
Category: B
Task: 1 (P-2)

Protective Gear:

Safety goggles or glasses with side shields

Describe the vehicle being worked on:

Year _____ Make _____ Model _____

VIN _____ Engine type and size _____

Describe general condition:
_____

PROCEDURE

Cylinder Head Removal

1. In an appropriate service manual, look up the sequence for loosening and removing the cylinder head bolts. In the space below, sketch the cylinder head and the number sequence for loosening and removing the bolts. If the manual does not illustrate the loosening sequence, reverse the installation sequence.   ☐ Task completed

2. Remove the valve cover or covers. If the engine has an overhead camshaft, remove it so that you have access to the cylinder head bolts (Figure 1). ☐ Task completed

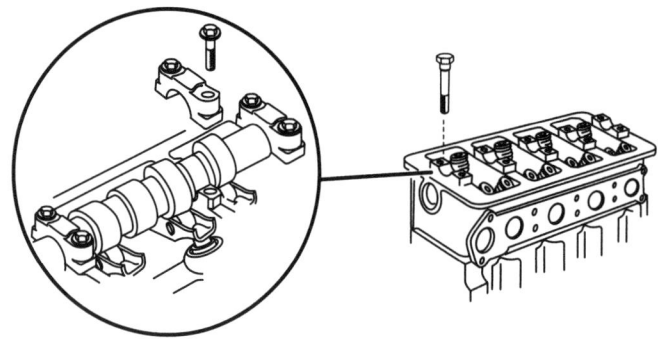

Figure 1. Removing an overhead camshaft.

3. Drain the coolant from the engine. Loosen and remove the cylinder head bolts. Make sure you refer to your drawing and bolt-loosening sequence. All of the bolts should be initially loosened one turn. Then remove the bolts and note the location of each on your drawing. This is important because some engines use head bolts with different lengths. ☐ Task completed

4. Remove the pushrods (if equipped) and place them in a fixture that will keep them in order. ☐ Task completed

5. Lift the cylinder head off the engine (Figure 2). Store the cylinder head gasket for later reference. ☐ Task completed

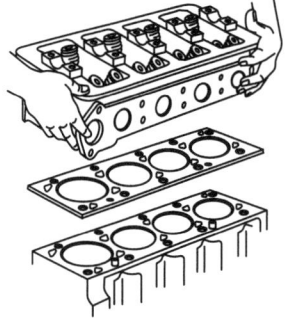

Figure 2. Removing a cylinder head.

Cylinder Head Disassembly

6. Place the head on a flat surface with the valve heads down. With a soft-faced hammer, tap on the valve spring retainers. This will make disassembly easier. ☐ Task completed

7. Adjust the jaws of a valve spring compressor so that they fit the spring retainers. Put the cylinder head on its side so that you have access to the valve head and stem. ☐ Task completed

   CAUTION: *Never use a valve spring compressor that has bent or distorted jaws. Also, make sure you are wearing safety glasses while removing the valves.*

8. Begin at one end of the cylinder head and remove the valve assemblies by compressing the valve spring and removing the valve locks (Figure 3). A small magnet makes removing the valve locks easier. ☐ Task completed

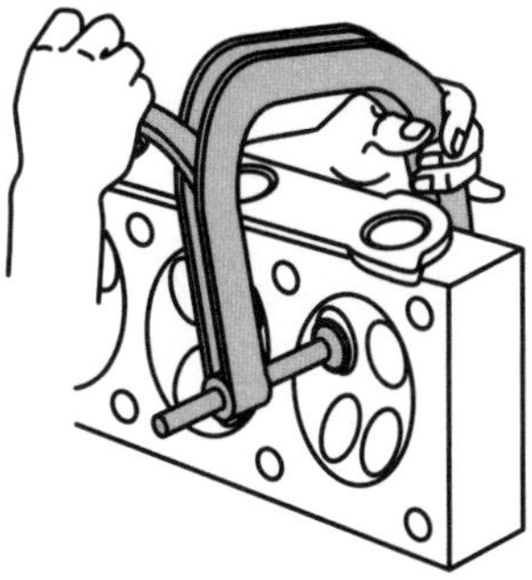

Figure 3. Using a valve spring compressor to remove the valve assembly.

9. Slowly release the spring compressor and remove it from the head. Collect the valve spring and spring retainer, then pull out the valve. ☐ Task completed

10. Arrange valve, spring, and washer in storage rack so they can be reinstalled in the same locations. ☐ Task completed

Problems Encountered

_____
_____
_____

Instructor's Comments

_____
_____
_____

☐ JOB SHEET / AT 101-6

Remove Cylinder Ring Ridge

Name _____ Station _____ Date _____

Objective

Upon completion of this job sheet, you will have demonstrated the ability to correctly use a ridge removal tool to remove a cylinder ring ridge. You must know how to perform this task in order to pass the ASE Engine Repair Test. Before beginning, review the appropriate material under the "Cylinder Block Disassembly" heading in **Chapter 9** of AUTOMOTIVE TECHNOLOGY.

These job sheets meet the requirements for **NATEF** task(s): **Engine Block Assembly Diagnosis and Repair.**

Tools and Materials:
AUTOMOTIVE TECHNOLOGY 4e (Thomson, Delmar Learning)
Oily shop towel
Ridge removal tool
Wrench

NATEF TASKS
I. Engine Repair
Category: C
Task: 4 (P-2)

Protective Gear:
Safety goggles or glasses with side shields

Describe the vehicle being worked on:
Year _____ Make _____ Model _____
VIN _____ Engine type and size _____

PROCEDURE

1. Rotate each piston to bottom dead center and inspect the cylinder to see if there is a ring ridge. Use your fingernail to inspect for a ridge. If it catches on the cylinder wall, the ridge must be removed. ☐ Task completed

2. Select the correct-size ridge reamer and position it in the cylinder with the piston at bottom dead center. Adjust the cutter against the cylinder walls according to the instructions furnished with the tool. ☐ Task completed

3. Use a wrench to turn the tool in a clockwise direction. ☐ Task completed

   WARNING: *Always wear safety goggles or glasses with side shields when completing this task.*

   Rotate the tool around the cylinder until the ridge is removed. Be careful not to remove more than the ridge.

   It is possible that all of the ridge may not be removed. Why is this?

   _____

   _____

   _____

4. Repeat this operation in each of the other cylinders. ☐ Task completed

5. Use an oily shop towel to remove the cuttings from each cylinder. ☐ Task completed

Problems Encountered

_____
_____
_____

Instructor's Comments

_____
_____
_____

SHOP ACTIVITY / AT 101-3

Engine Disassembly

Name _____ Station _____ Date _____

Objective

Upon completion of this activity, you will be able to explain the different disassembly procedures used by different manufacturers.

Refer to **Chapter 9** in the AUTOMOTIVE TECHNOLOGY book for additional information.

This Shop Activity meets the requirements for **NATEF** task(s): **General Engine Diagnosis; Removal and Reinstallation**

Tools and Materials:
AUTOMOTIVE TECHNOLOGY 4e (Thomson, Delmar Learning)
Service Manual
All-Data®

NATEF TASKS
I. Engine Repair
Category: A
Task: 2 (P-1)

Protective Gear:
N/A

Describe the vehicle being worked on: Vehicle #1
Year _____ Make _____ Model _____
VIN _____ Engine type and size _____

Describe the vehicle being worked on: Vehicle #2
Year _____ Make _____ Model _____
VIN _____ Engine type and size _____

PROCEDURE

Choose two V6 vehicles, each made by a different manufacturer, and compare the engine disassembly procedures given in their service literature. Describe the similarities and differences, and explain why there are differences.

A. Record disassembly procedures for Vehicle #1.

_____
_____
_____
_____

Engine Disassembly

B. Record disassembly procedures for Vehicle #2.

C. Describe the similarities between the two.

_____
_____
_____
_____
_____
_____
_____
_____

D. Describe the differences between the two.

_____
_____
_____
_____
_____
_____
_____
_____
_____

E. Explain the reasons for the differences in procedure between the two.

_____
_____
_____
_____

Problems Encountered

_____
_____
_____

Instructor's Comments

_____
_____
_____

Instructor's Signature

_____

SHOP ACTIVITY / AT 101-4

Cleaning Engine Parts

Name _____ Station _____ Date _____

Objective

Upon completion of this activity, you will be able to identify the types of equipment needed to clean the engine assembly and list the MSDS and possible health problems associated with the various chemicals used.

Refer to **Chapter 9** in the AUTOMOTIVE TECHNOLOGY book for additional information.

Tools and Materials:
AUTOMOTIVE TECHNOLOGY 4e (Thomson, Delmar Learning)
MSDS sheets

Protective Gear:
N/A

PROCEDURE

List all of the engine cleaning equipment and solvents that are available in your shop. When listing the solvents, include the health-related precautions listed on the solvent container's label or on its MSDS.

_____
_____
_____
_____
_____
_____
_____
_____
_____
_____
_____
_____

Problems Encountered

Instructor's Comments

Instructor's Signature

CASE STUDY

A technician is preparing to rebuild a 3.8-liter engine from a 2002 Buick. After removing the heads, what procedure should be performed before removing the pistons from the block, and why?

INFORMATION SHEET

Short Blocks

INFORMATION

These job sheets cover the inspection and service of an engine's short block. The short block is the basic mechanical unit of the engine, minus the cylinder head(s). While performing services to the short block, many precise measurements need to be taken. Make sure you know how to use and read a micrometer before proceeding with these job sheets.

A basic short block consists of the cylinder block, crankshaft, crankshaft bearings, connecting rods, connecting rod bearings, pistons and rings, and oil gallery and core plugs.

Cylinder Block

The cylinder block is normally a one-piece, cast block of metal machined so that all of the rotating parts fit properly.

The cylinder bores are the most critical part of the cylinder block. The walls of the cylinder bore must meet exact tolerances and be without flaws in order for the pistons to move freely up and down the bore.

Crankshaft

The crankshaft is housed in the engine block and is held in place by main bearing caps. Main bearings are placed between the main bearing caps, the crankshaft, and the cylinder block.

The crankshaft does not rotate directly on the bearings; rather, it rotates on a thin layer of engine oil trapped between the crankshaft journals and the bearing surface. The area that holds the oil is critical to engine durability. If the crankshaft journals become out of round, tapered, scored, or if the bearings are excessively worn, the proper oil film will not form. Without the proper oil film, premature engine wear will occur on the bearings and crankshaft journals. This can result in crankshaft breakage. The oil clearance is critical and must be measured carefully during engine inspection and overhaul.

Pistons

Combustion takes place between the top of the piston and the cylinder head. A piston is a can-shaped part that is closely fit into the cylinder. The gap between the outside of the piston and the cylinder walls is sealed by the piston rings. These rings are made from steel and are formed under tension so that they can expand out from the piston to the cylinder walls to form a good seal.

Making sure the piston is able to move freely up and down the cylinder wall while maintaining a seal is a critical task during engine overhaul.

☐ JOB SHEET / AT 101-7

Engine Block Inspection

Name _____   Station _____   Date _____

Objective

Upon completion of this job sheet, you will be able to inspect an engine block for visible cracks, check passage condition, check core and gallery plug condition, and detect surface warpage. You must know how to perform these tasks to pass the ASE Engine Repair Test. Before beginning, review **Chapter 8** of AUTOMOTIVE TECHNOLOGY.

These job sheets meet the requirements for **NATEF** task(s): **Engine Block Assembly Diagnosis and Repair.**

Tools and Materials:

AUTOMOTIVE TECHNOLOGY 4e (Thomson, Delmar Learning)

Tap set

Straightedge

Feeler gauge set

Miscellaneous wire brushes

NATEF TASKS
I. Engine Repair
Category: C
Task: 1 (P-2)
Task: 2 (P-2)
Task: 3 (P-2)

Protective Gear:

Goggles or safety glasses with side shields

Describe the vehicle being worked on:

Year _____   Make _____   Model _____

VIN _____   Engine type and size _____

PROCEDURE

1. Place the block in a position in which you can easily clean the threaded bores. This may involve rotating the block periodically while doing this.   ☐ Task completed

2. Run the correct-size tap through all threaded bores. Clean the tap after each use. Did you have a hard time running the tap through any bores?

   _____
   _____

3. Check to make sure the threads are in good condition. If they are not, they may need to be replaced. Record your findings and conclusions:

   _____
   _____

48 Short Blocks

4. Carefully look all around the block for evidence of coolant and/or oil leaks. Summarize your results:

   _____

   _____

   _____

5. Check the seal around each core and gallery plug. Are there signs of leakage? If so, what must be done?

   _____

   _____

   _____

6. Remove the core and gallery plugs. What types of plugs are used in this engine block? What did you need to do to remove the plugs?

   _____

   _____

   _____

7. After the plugs have been removed, inspect the sealing surface for the plugs and record their condition:

   _____

   _____

8. Run a properly sized wire brush through the water and oil passages. Make sure all debris is removed. ☐ Task completed

9. Carefully inspect the areas around all bores, threaded or non-threaded, for evidence of cracks. Summarize your results:

   _____

   _____

   _____

10. Place the straightedge diagonally across the deck surface. ☐ Task completed

11. The amount of warpage is determined by the size of feeler gauge you fit into the gap between the straightedge and the deck. What was the largest feeler gauge blade you could insert?

    _____

12. Move the straightedge to the other diagonal on the deck surface and repeat the above procedure. What was the largest feeler gauge blade you could insert?

    _____

13. How much warpage is there on the deck surface? What do you recommend?

   _____
   _____
   _____

14. After the block has been thoroughly inspected and cleaned, it is ready for further service and then assembly.   ☐ Task completed

Problems Encountered

_____
_____
_____

Instructor's Comments

_____
_____
_____

Short Blocks 51

☐ JOB SHEET / AT 101-8

Deglaze and Clean Cylinder Walls

Name _____ Station _____ Date _____

Objective

Upon completion of this job sheet, you will be able to deglaze and clean the cylinder walls in an engine block. You must know how to perform these tasks to pass the ASE Engine Repair Test. Before beginning, review **Chapter 8** of AUTOMOTIVE TECHNOLOGY.

These job sheets meet the requirements for **NATEF** task(s): **Engine Block Assembly Diagnosis and Repair.**

Tools and Materials:
AUTOMOTIVE TECHNOLOGY 4e (Thomson, Delmar Learning)
Glaze breaker
Variable-speed electric drill or honing machine
Large, round stiff-bristled brush
Clean lint-free cloth

NATEF TASKS
I. Engine Repair
Category: C
Task: 4 (P-2)
Task: 5 (P-2)

Protective Gear:
Goggles or safety glasses with side shields

Describe the vehicle being worked on:
Year _____ Make _____ Model _____
VIN _____ Engine type and size _____

PROCEDURE

1. Carefully inspect and measure the cylinder bores for surface condition, taper, and out-of-roundness. Record your findings here:

   _____
   _____
   _____

2. If the bores are within acceptable limits, the cylinder walls only need to be deglazed. What causes glaze on the cylinder walls?

   _____
   _____

3. State what you are going to use to spin the glaze breaker:

   _____
   _____

Problems Encountered

_____
_____
_____

Instructor's Comments

_____
_____
_____

Short Blocks   61

☐ JOB SHEET / AT 101-11

Measure Camshaft Lobes/Cam and Bearing Journals

Name _____ Station _____ Date _____

Objective

Upon completion of this job sheet, you will have demonstrated the ability to perform a camshaft evaluation by performing a series of precise measurements. Before beginning to do this job sheet, review the material on the topic in **Chapter 10** of AUTOMOTIVE TECHNOLOGY.

These job sheets meet the requirements for **NATEF** task(s): **Engine Block Assembly Diagnosis and Repair**

Tools and Materials:

AUTOMOTIVE TECHNOLOGY 4e (Thomson, Delmar Learning)

Outside micrometer

Service manual

NATEF TASKS
I. Engine Repair
Category: C
Task: 6 (P-3)

Protective Gear:

Safety goggles or glasses with side shields

Describe the engine being worked on:

Year _____ Make _____ Model _____

VIN _____ Engine type and size _____

PROCEDURE

1. Using a service manual, look up the specifications for standard camshaft size and tolerances for normal wear. Record these specifications on the Report Sheet for Measuring Camshaft Cam/Lobes and Bearing Journals (found at end of Job Sheet). ☐ Task completed

2. Inspect the camshaft for signs of case hardening failure; if found, discard the camshaft. ☐ Task completed

3. Use proper procedures to clean it before beginning the measurement process. ☐ Task completed

4. Using the proper size outside micrometer, inspect the front camshaft bearing journal twice at each end of the journal, once horizontal to the camshaft and once vertical. Record all of the measurements on the report sheet. (**Note:** *If these measurements are different, the camshaft bearing journal is out-of-round or tapered and the camshaft should be replaced.*) ☐ Task completed

5. Repeat step 3 for each of the remaining camshaft bearing journals. ☐ Task completed

6. Measure the first camshaft lobe three times at each end of the surface, once horizontally to the camshaft and twice vertically at each edge. Record all of the measurements on the report sheet. (**Note:** *The measurement difference between the horizontal and the vertical is the camshaft lift for that* ☐ Task completed

lobe.) Determine whether this lobe is an exhaust or intake, and record the measurements.

7. Repeat step 6 for each of the remaining exhaust and intake lobes.

8. Compare the measurements of the camshaft bearing journals with the specifications. Next compare the measurements of the camshaft lobes with those of the specifications to determine of the lobe. If the measurements are within specifications, the camshaft can be reinstalled in the engine. If the measurements are not within factory specifications, the camshaft must be replaced. ☐ Task completed

Problems Encountered

___

___

___

Instructor's Comments

___

___

___

Name _____ Station _____ Date _____

REPORT SHEET FOR MEASURING CAMSHAFT MEASUREMENTS							
Bearing Journal Number	1	2	3	4	5	6	7
Standard bearing journal size							
Actual journal size							
Taper limits							
Out-of-round limits							
Actual out-of-roundness							
Camshaft Lobe Number	1 in	1 ex	2 in	2 ex	3 in	3 ex	
Base circle measurement							
Base circle actual size							
Lobe nose size 1							
Lobe nose size 2							
Actual lobe nose size							
Taper limits							
Actual taper							

Conclusions and Recommendations _____

Camshaft Lobe Number	4 in	4 ex	5 in	5 ex	6 in	6 ex	
Base circle measurement							
Base circle actual size							
Lobe nose size 1							
Lobe nose size 2							
Actual lobe nose size							
Taper limits							
Actual taper							

Conclusions and Recommendations _____

☐ JOB SHEET / AT 101-12

Install Camshaft Bearings

Name _____ Station _____ Date _____

Objective

Upon completion of this job sheet, you will have demonstrated the ability to properly install camshaft bearings. You must know how to perform this task in order to pass the ASE Engine Repair Test. Before beginning, review the section under the "Camshaft Bearings" heading in **Chapter 10** of AUTOMOTIVE TECHNOLOGY.

These job sheets meet the requirements for **NATEF** task(s): **Engine Block Assembly Diagnosis and Repair**

Tools and Materials:
AUTOMOTIVE TECHNOLOGY 4e (Thomson, Delmar Learning)
Bearings
Heavy ball peen hammer
Light engine oil
Mandrel
Service manual
Short or long driving bar

NATEF TASKS
I. Engine Repair
Category: C
Task: 6 (P-3)

Protective Gear:
Goggles or safety glasses with side shields

Describe the engine being worked on:
Year _____ Make _____ Model _____
VIN _____ Engine type and size _____

PROCEDURE

Note: *Perform this task only if assigned by your instructor if inspection results warrant bearing replacement.*

1. Wipe the camshaft bores. Sort and lay out the new bearings in the correct order, from front to rear. Select either a short or long driving bar. Then select a mandrel closest to the cam bearing in size (Figure 6). ☐ Task completed

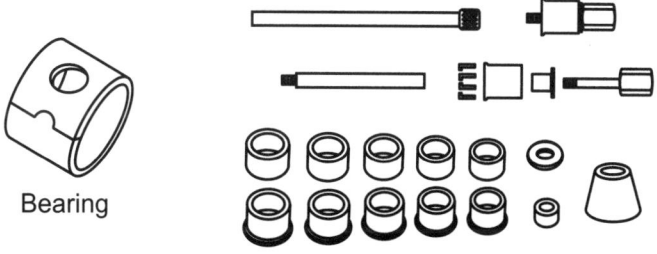

Bearing

Complete set

Figure 6. Selecting a mandrel that is closest in size to the cam bearing.

2. Place the bearing on the mandrel (it will fit loosely), and turn the bearing driver clockwise until the mandrel is snug in the bearing. Lubricate the bearing with light engine oil. ☐ Task completed

3. Start the bearing into the block by hand pressure (Figure 7). Make sure the oil passages align before driving the bearing into the block housing, and be sure to back off on the driving bar one-eighth turn. This will allow the 0.003- to 0.006-inch press fit. ☐ Task completed

Figure 7. Starting the bearing into the block with hand pressure.

4. Refer to the engine manufacturer's specifications for proper bearing positioning. Generally, the bearing will be seated correctly when the mandrel is flush with the face of the block (Figure 8). Some cam bearings must be installed further in the bore to align with the oil holes in the block. ☐ Task completed

Figure 8. A bearing is seated correctly when the mandrel is flush with the face of the block.

5. Drive the bearing into the block by using sharp blows with a heavy ball peen hammer (Figure 9). Make sure the oil holes in the bearing and block are aligned.　☐ Task completed

   WARNING: *Always wear eye protection whenever striking a driver bar with a hammer. Keep the driver bar dressed to prevent chips from flying off.*

   WARNING: *Make sure the hammer handle is properly wedged to the hammer head. Do not use a hammer with a loose handle.*

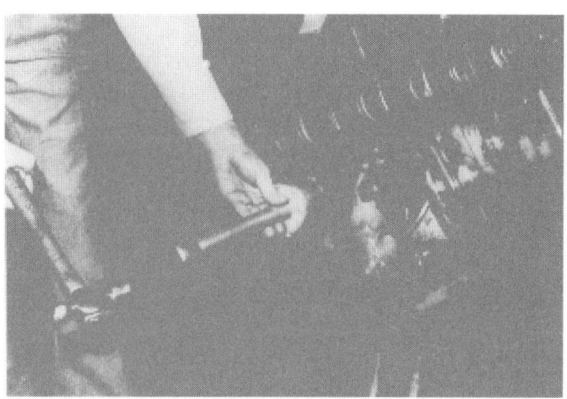

Figure 9. Driving a bearing into a block.

6. Remove the mandrel by withdrawing the driving bar. Check for any nicks or burrs on the bearing and remove, if present. Follow the same procedure for the remainder of the bearings.　☐ Task completed

Problems Encountered

_____
_____
_____

Instructor's Comments

_____
_____
_____

☐ JOB SHEET / AT 101-13

Inspect and Replace Camshaft Drives

Name _____ Station _____ Date _____

Objective

Upon completion of this job sheet, you will have demonstrated the ability to inspect and replace camshaft drives. You must know how to perform these tasks to pass the ASE Engine Repair Test. Before beginning, review the appropriate section under the "Timing Mechanisms" heading in **Chapter 10** of AUTOMOTIVE TECHNOLOGY.

These job sheets meet the requirements for **NATEF** task(s): **Engine Block Assembly Diagnosis and Repair**

Tools and Materials:
AUTOMOTIVE TECHNOLOGY 4e (Thomson, Delmar Learning)
Hand tools
Service manual

NATEF TASKS
I. Engine Repair
Category: B
Task: 12 (P-2)
Task: 13 (P-1)

Protective Gear:
Goggles or safety glasses with side shields

Describe the engine being worked on:
Year _____ Make _____ Model _____
VIN _____ Engine type and size _____

PROCEDURE

1. Disconnect the negative battery cable. ☐ Task completed
2. Remove the covers protecting the camshaft drive gears. ☐ Task completed
3. Inspect for proper alignment of the timing marks on the timing gears. ☐ Task completed
4. Remove the timing gears according to the service manual. ☐ Task completed
5. Clean the timing gears. ☐ Task completed
6. Inspect the gears for wear or cracks, and replace necessary parts. ☐ Task completed
7. After replacing any worn or damaged gears and drives, set the timing marks according to the service manual. ☐ Task completed
8. Rotate the engine through two complete rotations of the crankshaft. Check to see if the timing marks on the gears are still in proper alignment. ☐ Task completed
9. Reinstall all covers removed for access. ☐ Task completed

10. Reconnect the negative battery cable and start the engine. ☐ Task completed

11. Set the ignition timing to the manufacturer's specifications. ☐ Task completed

Problems Encountered
_____
_____
_____

Instructor's Comments
_____
_____
_____

☐ JOB SHEET / AT 101-15

Checking and Servicing Pistons and Pins

Name _____ Station _____ Date _____

Objective

Upon completion of this job sheet, you will be able to inspect, measure, and service pistons and pins. You must know how to perform these tasks to pass the ASE Engine Repair Test. Before beginning, review **Chapter 8** of AUTOMOTIVE TECHNOLOGY.

These job sheets meet the requirements for **NATEF** task(s): **Engine Block Assembly Diagnosis and Repair**

Tools and Materials:

AUTOMOTIVE TECHNOLOGY 4e (Thomson, Delmar Learning)

Scraper
Cold tank
Ring groove cleaner
Small hydraulic press
Variety of drivers and adapters
Feeler gauge

NATEF TASKS
I. Engine Repair
Category: C
Task: 9 (P-3)
Task: 10 (P-2)
Task: 11 (P-3)

Protective Gear:

Goggles or safety glasses with side shields

Describe the engine being worked on:

Year _____ Make _____ Model _____

VIN _____ Engine type and size _____

PROCEDURE

1. Thoroughly remove the carbon from the top of the pistons. Be careful not to remove any metal from the piston. What did you need to do in order to get the carbon off?

   _____
   _____

2. Remove the piston rings. Clean and inspect the ring grooves. Make sure all of the openings at the rear of the grooves are free of carbon and/or debris. ☐ Task completed

3. After the piston is cleaned, determine if the piston is offset on the rod. If so, what mark did the manufacturer use to indicate the direction of installation? If the piston is offset from the rod and there are no markings, make some. What could you use to do that?

   _____
   _____

4. Examine the piston pin and describe how it is retained. Describe that here:

   _____

   _____

5. Remove the piston from the rod according to the type of piston pin used   ☐ Task completed

   Full-Floating Pins

   a. Remove the snap rings from the pin boss. Note the direction the snap rings were installed in the boss. Describe that here:

      _____

      _____

   b. Push the pin out of the piston and connecting rod. Did you have any difficulty pushing the pin out?

      _____

   c. Carefully inspect the snap ring groove. Record your findings:

      _____

      _____

   Press-Fit Pins

   a. Set the correct-size lower adapter onto the base of the press and place the piston and rod assembly on it. Does the adapter support the piston and will it allow enough room for the pin as it is pressed out?

      _____

   b. Choose the correct driver and set it into the pin. Does the driver fully contact the pin and will it clear the pin bore as the pin is pressed out?

      _____

   c. Press the pin out and separate the rod from the piston.   ☐ Task completed

   d. Examine the piston pin bore and describe the condition.

      _____

      _____

6. Visually inspect the piston head for any damage, then describe its condition.

   _____

   _____

7. Visually inspect the piston skirts for indications of scuffing. What did you find?

   _____

   _____

8. Measure the ring groove for wear by inserting a new piston ring backward in the groove and measure the clearance between the groove and the ring with a feeler gauge. The measurement was: _____

9. Compare this reading with the specifications. The specifications are: _____ What does this indicate?

_____

_____

10. Measure the bore for the piston pin and compare your reading to the specifications. Your measurement was: _____ The specifications call for a bore of: _____ Is there a difference and, if so, what does that indicate?

_____

_____

11. Check the bore for taper, out-of-roundness, and parallelism. How did you do that?

_____

_____

12. Visually inspect the piston pin and record your observations.

_____

_____

13. Measure the diameter of the piston pin and compare your reading to the specifications. Your measurement was: _____ The specifications call for a bore of: _____ Is there a difference and, if so, what does that indicate?

_____

_____

14. Inspect the small bore of the connecting rod and record the results of the inspection.

_____

_____

15. Measure the inside diameter of the small bore and compare your reading to the specifications. Your measurement was: _____ The specifications call for a bore of: _____ Is there a difference, and, if so, what does that indicate?

_____

_____

16. Check the bore for taper, out-of-roundness, and parallelism. How did you do that?

   _____

   _____

17. Replace or recondition any part that needs to be. What parts need to be serviced prior to assembling the rod and piston?

   _____

   _____

Problems Encountered

_____
_____
_____

Instructor's Comments

_____
_____
_____

☐ JOB SHEET / AT 101-16

Install Pistons and Connecting Rods

Name _____ Station _____ Date _____

Objective

Upon completion of this job sheet, you will have demonstrated the ability to properly install pistons and connecting rods. You must know how to perform these tasks in order to pass the ASE Engine Repair Test. Before beginning, review the section under the "Installing Pistons and Connecting Rods" heading in **Chapter 10** of AUTOMOTIVE TECHNOLOGY.

These job sheets meet the requirements for **NATEF** task(s): **Engine Block Assembly Diagnosis and Repair**

Tools and Materials:

AUTOMOTIVE TECHNOLOGY 4e (Thomson, Delmar Learning)
Allen wrench
Anaerobic thread-locking compound
Compressor tool
Feeler gauges
Flat-blade screwdriver
Light engine oil
Plastic mallet
Plastigage
Rubber or aluminum protectors or guides
Service manual

NATEF TASKS
I. Engine Repair
Category: C
Task: 12 (P-1)

Protective Gear:

Goggles or safety glasses with side shields

Describe the engine being worked on:

Year _____ Make _____ Model _____
VIN _____ Engine type and size _____

PROCEDURE

1. Place rubber or aluminum protectors or guides over the threaded section of the rod bolts. Lightly coat the piston, rings, cylinder wall, crankpin, and compressor tool with light engine oil. Do not coat the rod bearings with oil at this time. ☐ Task completed

2. Be sure that the ring gaps are located on the piston in the positions recommended in the service manual. ☐ Task completed

3. Expand the compressor tool around the piston rings. Position the steps on the compressor tool downward. Tighten the compressor tool with an Allen wrench to compress the piston rings. ☐ Task completed

4. Rotate the crankshaft until the crankpin is at its lowest level (BDC). Place the piston/rod assembly into the cylinder bore until the steps on the compressor tool contact the cylinder block deck. Make sure the piston reference mark is in the correct relation to the front of the engine. ☐ Task completed

80 Short Blocks

5. Remove the protective covering from the rod bolts. Lightly tap on the head of the piston with a mallet handle or block of wood until piston enters the cylinder bore. ☐ Task completed

6. Push the piston down the bore while making sure the connecting rod fits into place on the crankpin. ☐ Task completed

7. Using a service manual, locate the oil clearance specification for the connecting rod bearings and torque specifications for the cap bolts. Record these specifications on the Report Sheet for Installing Connecting Rods and Pistons. ☐ Task completed

8. Determine the rod bearing oil clearance using the Plastigage in the same manner as when checking the oil clearance for main bearings. Record the results on the Report Sheet for Installing Connecting Rods and Pistons. If out of specification, consult with your instructor. ☐ Task completed

9. Remove all of the cap bolts and push the piston rod assembly a slight distance from crankshaft. Lubricate all bearings with light engine oil. ☐ Task completed

10. Seat the connecting rod yoke onto the crankshaft. Apply a drop of anaerobic thread-locking compound to each thread of the rod bolts. ☐ Task completed

11. Position the matching connecting rod cap and finger-tighten the rod nuts. Make sure the connecting rod blade and cap markings are on the same side. Gently tap each cap with a plastic mallet as it is being installed to properly position and seat it. ☐ Task completed

12. Torque the rod nuts to specifications. ☐ Task completed

    CAUTION: *Use new nuts, because they are self-locking.*

13. Repeat the piston/rod assembly procedure for each assembly. ☐ Task completed

14. Using a service manual, locate the connecting rod side clearance specification. Record this specification on the Report Sheet for Installing Connecting Rods and Pistons. ☐ Task completed

15. Measure the side clearance by spreading the connecting rods with a large, flat-blade screwdriver. Measure the clearance with feeler gauge. ☐ Task completed

Problems Encountered

_____
_____
_____

Instructor's Comments

_____
_____
_____

SHOP ACTIVITY / AT 101-5

Crankshaft

Name _____ Station _____ Date _____

Objective

Upon completion of this activity, you will be able to correctly identify the various parts of a crankshaft.

Refer to **Chapter 10** in the AUTOMOTIVE TECHNOLOGY book for additional information.

Tools and Materials:
AUTOMOTIVE TECHNOLOGY 4e (Thomson, Delmar Learning)
Automotive Crankshaft

Protective Gear:
N/A

Describe the vehicle being worked on:
Year _____ Make _____ Model _____
VIN _____ Engine type and size _____

PROCEDURE

Using an instructor-designated crankshaft, identify the various parts and record your findings. Note any irregularities you may see.

_____
_____
_____
_____
_____
_____
_____
_____
_____
_____
_____
_____
_____
_____
_____

Problems Encountered

Instructor's Comments

Instructor's Signature

SHOP ACTIVITY / AT 101-6

Pistons

Name _____ Station _____ Date _____

Objective

Upon completion of this activity, you will correctly identify the various parts of a piston.

Refer to **Chapter 10** in the AUTOMOTIVE TECHNOLOGY book for additional information.

Tools and Materials:

AUTOMOTIVE TECHNOLOGY 4e (Thomson, Delmar Learning)

Automotive piston

Instructor notes

Protective Gear:

Safety Glasses

NATEF TASKS
I. Engine Repair
Category: C
Task: 8 (P-2)

PROCEDURE

Using an instructor-designated piston, identify the various parts and record your findings. Note any irregularities you may see.

_____
_____
_____
_____
_____
_____
_____
_____
_____
_____
_____
_____
_____
_____

Problems Encountered

Instructor's Comments

Instructor's Signature

SHOP ACTIVITY / AT 101-7

Pistons

Name _____ Station _____ Date _____

Objective

Upon completion of this activity, you will be able to demonstrate the ability to remove piston rings using the proper tools.

Refer to **Chapter 10** in the AUTOMOTIVE TECHNOLOGY book for additional information.

Tools and Materials:

AUTOMOTIVE TECHNOLOGY 4e (Thomson, Delmar Learning)

Automotive piston

Piston ring expanding tool

Protective Gear:

Safety Glasses

NATEF TASKS
I. Engine Repair
Category: C
Task: 12 (P-1)

PROCEDURE

Using an instructor-designated piston, carefully remove the piston rings using a ring expander. Do not attempt this procedure without this tool. Be careful not to expand the ring any more than necessary, and be sure to wear eye protection. Have your instructor inspect your work.

Problems Encountered

_____
_____
_____

Instructor's Comments

_____
_____
_____

Instructor's Signature

_____

SHOP ACTIVITY / AT 101-8

Pistons

Name _____ Station _____ Date _____

Objective

Upon completion of this activity, you will be able to demonstrate the ability to clean piston ring grooves using the proper tools.

Refer to **Chapter 10** in the AUTOMOTIVE TECHNOLOGY book for additional information.

Tools and Materials:
AUTOMOTIVE TECHNOLOGY 4e (Thomson, Delmar Learning)
Automotive piston
Piston ring groove cleaner

Protective Gear:
Safety Glasses

PROCEDURE

Using an instructor-designated piston, carefully clean the piston ring grooves using a ring groove cleaner. Do not attempt this procedure without this tool. Be careful not to gouge the piston; only the carbon should be removed. Be sure to wear eye protection. Have your instructor inspect your work.

Problems Encountered

_____
_____
_____

Instructor's Comments

_____
_____
_____

Instructor's Signature

_____

SHOP ACTIVITY / AT 101-9

Pistons

Name _____ Station _____ Date _____

Objective

Upon completion of this activity, you will be able to demonstrate the ability to install piston rings on a piston using the proper tools and procedures.

Refer to **Chapter 10** in the AUTOMOTIVE TECHNOLOGY book for additional information.

Tools and Materials:

AUTOMOTIVE TECHNOLOGY 4e (Thomson, Delmar Learning)

Automotive piston

Piston ring expander

U.S.C. feeler gauge

Service manual

NATEF TASKS
I. Engine Repair
Category: C
Task: 12 (P-1)

Protective Gear:

Safety Glasses

PROCEDURE

Using an instructor-designated piston, carefully reinstall the piston rings using the ring expander. Do not attempt this procedure without this tool. Be careful not to expand the ring larger than necessary or it will break. After installing the rings, measure ring end gap and ring side clearance following service manual procedures. Be sure to wear eye protection. Have your instructor inspect your work when done.

Problems Encountered

_____
_____
_____

Instructor's Comments

_____
_____
_____

Instructor's Signature

_____

INFORMATION SHEET

Cylinder Heads and Valves

INFORMATION

These jobs sheets cover the services generally performed to the cylinder head and valves during an engine overhaul. Also included are those services that may be performed to other parts of the engine while performing an overhaul.

The cylinder head mounts on the top of the engine block and serves as the uppermost seal for the combustion chamber. To aid in that sealing, a head gasket is sandwiched between the cylinder head and the upper deck of the engine block. The head also contains the valves that must open and close to allow the air/fuel mixture to come in and allow exhaust gases to escape. The cylinder head may also be the mounting point for the camshaft.

Much of the work done to the cylinder head and valves is done to ensure a good seal. The cylinder head and valves are another area where the ability to use precision measurements is essential.

Cylinder Heads and Valves   97

☐ JOB SHEET / AT 101-17

Inspect Cylinder Head for Wear

Name _____ Station _____ Date _____

Objective

Upon completion of this job sheet, you will have demonstrated the ability to check a cylinder head for flatness, inspect it for cracks, and measure stem-to-guide clearance. You must know how to perform these tasks in order to pass the ASE Engine Repair Test. Before beginning, review the section under the "Valve Guide Reconditioning" heading in **Chapter 11** of AUTOMOTIVE TECHNOLOGY.

These job sheets meet the requirements for **NATEF** task(s): **Cylinder Head and Valve Train Diagnosis and Repair**

Tools and Materials:

AUTOMOTIVE TECHNOLOGY 4e (Thomson, Delmar Learning)

Dial indicator

Dye penetrant or magnetic inspection equipment

Feeler gauge

Micrometer

Service manual

Straightedge

Telescoping gauge/small-hole gauge

NATEF TASKS
I. Engine Repair
Category: B
Task: 1 (P-2)
Task: 5 (P-3)

Protective Gear:

Goggles or safety glasses with side shields

Describe the engine being worked on:

Year _____ Make _____ Model _____

VIN _____ Engine type and size _____

Describe general condition: _____

PROCEDURE

1. Look up the specifications for stem-to-guide clearance for your engine and record them on the Report Sheet for Cylinder Head Inspection (found on page 101). ☐ Task completed

2. Look up the specification for maximum warpage limit for your engine and record it on the Report Sheet for Cylinder Head Inspection. ☐ Task completed

3. Perform a visual inspection of the cylinder head. Report your findings on the Report Sheet for Cylinder Head Inspection. ☐ Task completed

4. Position a straightedge over the cylinder head's sealing surface. Try to slide a feeler gauge strip the size of the maximum limit under any part of the straightedge (Figure 12). If the feeler gauge goes under the straightedge, the cylinder head is warped. Record the results on the Report Sheet for Cylinder Head Inspection. If the head is warped, check with your instructor. ☐ Task completed

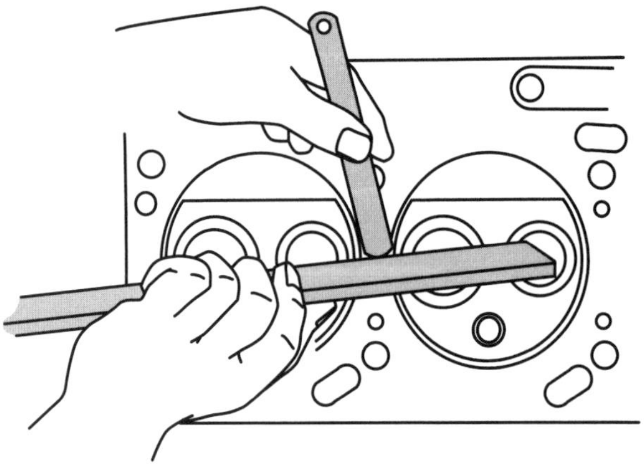

Figure 12. Measuring the flatness of the surface of a cylinder head.

5. Use a dye penetrant or magnetic inspection equipment to look for cracks in the cylinder head around the valve seats. If you find a crack, notify your instructor. ☐ Task completed

6. To measure valve stem guides, first make sure the guides are clean. Install a small hole gauge or telescoping gauge into one of the guides and expand it. Remove the gauge and measure it with an outside micrometer. Measure the guide in three places: top, middle, and bottom. Note your largest reading on the Report Sheet for Cylinder Head Inspection. ☐ Task completed

7. From your storage tray, select a valve that fits in this guide. Use an outside micrometer to measure the part of the stem that rides in the guide. Take measurements in three places: top, middle, and bottom. Note your smallest reading on the Report Sheet for Cylinder Head Inspection. ☐ Task completed

8. The clearance for this guide is found by comparing the largest guide measurement with the smallest stem measurement. Subtract the stem measurement from the guide measurement. Record the clearance on the Report Sheet for Cylinder Head Inspection. ☐ Task completed

9. Repeat this procedure for each valve guide, and record your results on the Report Sheet for Cylinder Head Inspection. ☐ Task completed

10. If you wish to use a dial indicator to check the clearance, mount the dial indicator on cylinder head (Figure 13). ☐ Task completed

Figure 13. Measuring valve guide clearance with dial indicator.

11. Place a valve that fits in the guide into the guide, and adjust the dial indicator to contact the valve head. Zero the dial indicator. Rock the valve against the dial indicator. The indicator will show the clearance. ☐ Task completed

12. Repeat this operation for each valve and record the results on the Report Sheet for Cylinder Head Inspection. Compare your clearance readings to the specifications to determine whether the valve guides require servicing. ☐ Task completed

Problems Encountered

_____
_____
_____

Instructor's Comments

_____
_____
_____

Name _____ Station _____ Date _____

REPORT SHEET FOR CYLINDER HEAD INSPECTION

1. Visual inspection

	Serviceable	Not serviceable
Threaded holes		
Core-hole plugs		
Machined surfaces		
Rocker studs or pedestal		
Water jackets		

Conclusions and Recommendations _____
_____

2. Head warpage
Specified limit _____
Actual _____

3. Valve stem and guide clearance specification
Intake valve _____
Exhaust valve _____

Cylinder		Guide	Stem	Clearance
1.	Intake			
	Exhaust			
2.	Intake			
	Exhaust			
3.	Intake			
	Exhaust			
4.	Intake			
	Exhaust			
5.	Intake			
	Exhaust			
6.	Intake			
	Exhaust			
7.	Intake			
	Exhaust			
8.	Intake			
	Exhaust			

Conclusions and Recommendations _____
_____

Cylinder Heads and Valves

☐ **JOB SHEET / AT 101-18**

Inspect and Test Valve Springs for Squareness, Pressure, and Free Height Comparison

Name _____ Station _____ Date _____

Objective

Upon completion of this job sheet, you will be able to test valve springs for squareness, pressure, and free height. You must know how to perform these tasks to pass the ASE Engine Repair Test. Before beginning, review the section under the "Valve Springs" heading in **Chapter 11** of AUTOMOTIVE TECHNOLOGY.

These job sheets meet the requirements for **NATEF** task(s): **Cylinder Head and Valve Train Diagnosis and Repair**

Tools and Materials:

AUTOMOTIVE TECHNOLOGY 4e (Thomson, Delmar Learning)
Straightedge
Square
Valve spring pressure tester
Feeler gauge
Service manual

NATEF TASKS
I. Engine Repair
Category: B
Task: 3 (P-2)

Protective Gear:

Goggles or safety glasses with side shields

Describe the engine being worked on:

Year _____ Make _____ Model _____

VIN _____ Engine type and size _____

Describe general condition:

_____

PROCEDURE

1. Clean all of the valve springs. ☐ Task completed

2. Visually inspect all of the valve springs for cracks or signs of wear. ☐ Task completed

3. Perform a squareness test: Set a spring upright against a square. Turn the spring until a gap appears between the spring and the square. Measure the gap with a feeler gauge. If the gap is greater than 0.060 inch (1.52 mm), the spring should be replaced. ☐ Task completed

4. Perform a spring pressure test: Refer to the service manual for proper spring pressure at the test height. Use the spring tester to test each spring for proper pressure at test height. Any spring that does not meet specifications should be replaced. ☐ Task completed

5. Perform a freestanding height test: Line up all of the valve springs on a flat surface. Place a straight edge across the tops of the springs. Any height discrepancy will be obvious. There should be no more than 1/16-inch (1.59 mm) of variance between the heights of the valves. ☐ Task completed

6. Measure the height of the shortest and the tallest valve spring and compare those measurements to the specifications. Based on the results of this measurement, you should be able to determine which other valves should be measured. Replace any spring that is not within specifications. ☐ Task completed

Problems Encountered

_____
_____
_____

Instructor's Comments

_____
_____
_____

☐ JOB SHEET / AT 101-19

Inspecting Valve Spring Retainers, Locks, and Valve Lock Grooves

Name _____ Station _____ Date _____

Objective

Upon completion of this job sheet, you will have demonstrated the ability to inspect valve spring retainers, locks, and valve lock grooves for excessive wear. You must know how to perform these tasks to pass the ASE Engine Repair Test. Before beginning, review the section under "Valve Spring Retainers and Keepers" heading in **Chapter 11** of AUTOMOTIVE TECHNOLOGY.

These job sheets meet the requirements for **NATEF** task(s): **Cylinder Head and Valve Train Diagnosis and Repair**

Tools and Materials:
AUTOMOTIVE TECHNOLOGY 4e (Thomson, Delmar Learning)

Protective Gear:
Goggles or safety glasses with side shields

NATEF TASKS
I. Engine Repair
Category: B
Task: 4 (P-2)

Describe the engine being worked on:

Year _____ Make _____ Model _____

VIN _____ Engine type and size _____

Describe general condition:

_____

PROCEDURE

1. Clean all of the retainers, locks, and valve stems. ☐ Task completed

2. Visually inspect the valve spring retainers, locks, and valve lock grooves (on the stem of the valves). ☐ Task completed

3. Install the locks in the lock grooves on the valve stems and move the lock around in the grooves to be sure there is still a proper (tight) fit. ☐ Task completed

4. If there is any sign of looseness or wear, replace the defective component. ☐ Task completed

Problems Encountered

_____
_____
_____

Instructor's Comments

☐ JOB SHEET / AT 101-20

Recondition Valve Faces

Name _____ Station _____ Date _____

Objective

Upon completion of this job sheet, you will have demonstrated the ability to properly grind valve faces. You must know how to perform these tasks in order to pass the ASE Engine Repair Test. Before beginning, review the section under the "Grinding Valves" heading in **Chapter 11** of AUTOMOTIVE TECHNOLOGY.

These job sheets meet the requirements for **NATEF** task(s): **Cylinder Head and Valve Train Diagnosis and Repair.**

Tools and Materials:
AUTOMOTIVE TECHNOLOGY 4e (Thomson, Delmar Learning)
Measuring scale
Service manual
Valve grinder

NATEF TASKS
I. Engine Repair
Category: B
Task: 6 (P-3)
Task: 7 (P-3)

Protective Gear:
Goggles or safety glasses with side shields

Describe the engine being worked on:
Year _____ Make _____ Model _____
VIN _____ Engine type and size _____
Describe general condition:
_____

PROCEDURE

1. Locate the following specifications in the service manual for this engine and record them: ☐ Task completed

   Intake valve face angle   _____
   Exhaust valve face angle   _____
   Intake valve minimum margin   _____
   Exhaust valve minimum margin   _____

2. Mount the stem of one of the valves in the V-bracket of the valve grinder. Turn on the machine and adjust the coolant flow over the grinding wheel.   ☐ Task completed

   WARNING: *Always wear safety goggles or glasses with side shields when completing this task.*

3. Advance the valve stem toward the wheel and grind just enough material off the stem to resurface it.   ☐ Task completed

4. Install the valve stem in the fixture and chamfer the tip.   ☐ Task completed

5. Repeat the stem dressing operation for each valve.   ☐ Task completed

6. Adjust the valve grinding chuck to the correct angle to grind the valves. Inspect the valve-face grinding stone. If it appears to require truing, discuss findings with your instructor.   ☐ Task completed

7. Adjust the chuck sleeve and chuck stop to accept the valve stems. Install a valve in the chuck and adjust the carriage plate stop to prevent the valve neck from contacting the grinding wheel.   ☐ Task completed

8. Turn on the grinder and adjust the coolant flow over the grinding wheel. Move the valve into grinding position and slowly bring the wheel into contact with it. Move the valve back and forth over the grinding wheel. Be sure not to let the valve face pass beyond the edge of the grinding wheel.   ☐ Task completed

9. Move the grinding wheel toward the valve in small increments until the face is smooth and shiny all the way around. Be careful to remove the minimum amount of metal. Back the grinding wheel away from the valve and then move the valve carriage back, out of the way.   ☐ Task completed

10. Use a 1/64″ (.40 mm) measuring scale to determine whether the margin is still an acceptable width (Figure 14).   ☐ Task completed

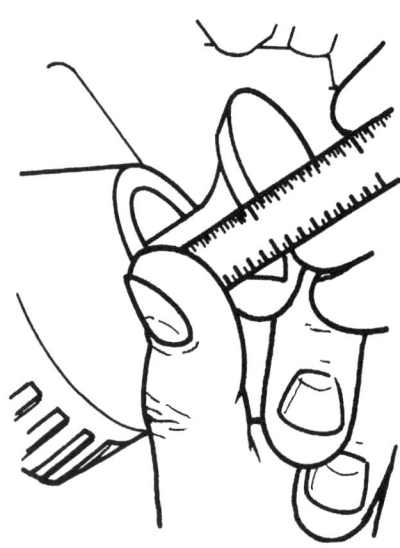

Figure 14. Measuring valve margin.

11. Grind each of the other valves and record the margin measurements in the spaces below. Valves with thin margins must be replaced. ☐ Task completed

Cylinder Number	Intake	Exhaust
1	_____	_____
2	_____	_____
3	_____	_____
4	_____	_____
5	_____	_____
6	_____	_____
7	_____	_____
8	_____	_____

Conclusions and Recommendations

_____
_____
_____

Problems Encountered

_____
_____
_____

Instructor's Comments

_____
_____
_____

CASE STUDY

A customer brings her 2002 Neon into the shop and complains that the engine is using too much oil. She presents a log of when oil was added. The log certainly verifies her complaint. The technician carefully inspects the engine for leaks and finds none. What should she do next?

_____
_____
_____
_____

Cylinder Heads and Valves

☐ JOB SHEET / AT 101-21

Inspect Valve Lifters, Pushrods, and Rocker Arms

Name _____ Station _____ Date _____

Objective

Upon completion of this job sheet, you will have demonstrated the ability to properly inspect valve lifters, pushrods, and rocker arms. You must know how to perform these tasks in order to pass the ASE Engine Repair Test. Before beginning, review the appropriate section under the "Camshaft and Valve Train Inspection" heading in **Chapter 10** of AUTOMOTIVE TECHNOLOGY.

These job sheets meet the requirements for **NATEF** task(s): **Cylinder Head and Valve Train Diagnosis and Repair**

Tools and Materials:

AUTOMOTIVE TECHNOLOGY 4e (Thomson, Delmar Learning)

Inside and outside micrometer Service manual

Leakdown tester Small, flat-blade screwdriver or pick

Rocker-arm grinding attachment Surface plate

NATEF TASKS
I. Engine Repair
Category: B
Task: 9 (P-2)
Task: 10 (P-2)

Protective Gear:

Goggles or safety glasses with side shields

Describe the engine being worked on:

Year _____ Make _____ Model _____

VIN _____ Engine type and size _____

PROCEDURE

1. Visually inspect each valve lifter where it contacts camshaft lobe. If you find any signs of wear, check with your instructor. ☐ Task completed

2. With your finger or a pushrod, firmly press down on the plunger of the lifter. Make sure it moves freely and with some resistance. If there is no movement or if the plunger moves easily, replace the lifter. ☐ Task completed

3. Roll each pushrod across a surface plate or drill press table. Inspect oil passage of each pushrod and the tips for galling and wear. ☐ Task completed

4. Visually inspect the contact area and bearing surface of each rocker arm. ☐ Task completed

5. Recondition the contact surface of cast rocker arm with the rocker-arm grinding attachment of a valve grinder. ☐ Task completed

   WARNING: *Always wear safety goggles or glasses with side shields when working around moving machinery and be sure that clothing is not loose.*

112 Cylinder Heads and Valves

6. If your engine has a rocker shaft, look for evidence of wear in the area where the rocker arm fits. Use inside and outside micrometers to determine the clearance between the rocker shaft and rocker arm. Compare the measurement to specifications. If the clearance is excessive, the rocker arms, shaft, or bushing may have to be replaced. Check with your instructor. ☐ Task completed

Problems Encountered

_____
_____
_____

Instructor's Comments

_____
_____
_____

Cylinder Heads and Valves 113

☐ JOB SHEET / AT 101-22

Valve Seat Reconditioning

Name _____ Station _____ Date _____

Objective

Upon completion of this job sheet, you will have demonstrated the ability to perform valve seat reconditioning. Before beginning this job sheet, review the material on the topic in Chapter 11 of AUTOMOTIVE TECHNOLOGY.

These job sheets meet the requirements for **NATEF** task(s): **Cylinder Head and Valve Train Diagnosis and Repair**

Tools and Materials:
AUTOMOTIVE TECHNOLOGY 4e (Thomson, Delmar Learning)
Measuring scale
Service manual
Valve seat cutter
Air nozzle
Compressed air

NATEF TASKS
I. Engine Repair
Category: B
Task: 7 (P-3)
Task: 6 (P-3)

Protective Gear:
Goggles or safety glasses with side shields
Safety boots

Describe the engine being worked on:
Year _____ Make _____ Model _____
VIN _____ Engine type and size _____
Describe the general condition:
_____

PROCEDURE

1. Locate the following specifications in the service manual for this engine and record them:

    Intake valve seat angle   _____
    Top narrowing angle   _____
    Bottom narrowing angle   _____
    Exhaust valve seat angle   _____
    Top narrowing angle   _____
    Bottom narrowing angle   _____

2. Mount cylinder head in holding fixture with valve chambers facing up. ☐ Task completed
3. Ensure valve seats and valve guides are clean and ready for the valve seat cutting process. ☐ Task completed
4. Insert pilot shaft into the valve guide, twisting slightly until snug. The pilot should not contact the valve guide. ☐ Task completed
5. Select the correct valve seat cutter for the exhaust valve seat. ☐ Task completed
6. Select the correct size and angle cutter and place seat cutter onto the valve pilot shaft and lower it onto valve seat. ☐ Task completed
7. Attach arbor "T" handle over the hex shape of the cutter. ☐ Task completed
8. Apply light pressure to "T" handle, and rotate the valve seat cutter clockwise two or three complete revolutions. The light downward pressure needs to be centered over the seat cutter. ☐ Task completed
9. Remove the seat cutter from the pilot shaft. ☐ Task completed
10. Give a short blast of compressed air onto the valve seat to remove cuttings. ☐ Task completed
11. Visually inspect for a shiny pit-free concentric valve seat. ☐ Task completed
12. Measure the width of the valve seat using measuring scale. ☐ Task completed
13. Remove the valve seat cutter pilot shaft. ☐ Task completed
14. Chalk the valve face of the exhaust valve for this location in the head. ☐ Task completed
15. Install the exhaust valve into the valve guide and lower the valve face onto its seat. ☐ Task completed
16. Placing light thumb pressure on the valve head rotate it back and forth approximately 30 degrees. ☐ Task completed
17. Remove the valve from the valve guide, and inspect the valve face for the valve seat contact location. ☐ Task completed
18. As a general rule, the valve seat contact should be centered on the valve face surface and one-half the width of the valve face. If the valve seat meets the valve face position criteria, the valve seat reconditioning is complete for this valve. ☐ Task completed

    NOTE: *If the valve face is too wide, then a top narrowing and bottom narrowing of the valve seat is required.*

Bottom Narrowing of the Seat

1. Select the bottoming narrowing cutter. ☐ Task completed
2. Insert the pilot shaft into the valve guide until snug; place the selected narrowing cutter on the pilot shaft. ☐ Task completed
3. Exerting a light downward pressure, cut the bottom of the seat until a continuous fine line forms with the valve seat. This process raises the bottom edge of the valve seat. ☐ Task completed

Top Narrowing of the Seat

1. Select the top narrowing cutter. ☐ Task completed
2. Insert pilot shaft into the valve guide until snug, place the selected narrowing cutter on the pilot shaft. ☐ Task completed
3. Exerting a light downward pressure, cut the top of the seat until a continuous fine line forms, and the valve seat is slightly less than its required width. This process lowers the top edge of the valve seat, and the seat is ready for the final cut. ☐ Task completed

Finish Cut of the Valve Seat

1. Proceed with the final cutting of the valve seat; follow steps 6 through 17 above. Once this valve seat is completed, follow the above process to cut the remaining exhaust valve seats in the head(s). ☐ Task completed

2. To cut the intake valve seats, use the same procedure as for the exhaust valves, except the valve seat cutter for the intake valves will be larger in diameter. ☐ Task completed

Problems Encountered

_____
_____
_____

Instructor's Comments

_____
_____
_____

Cylinder Heads and Valves 117

☐ JOB SHEET / AT 101-23

Install Cylinder Heads and Gaskets

Name _____ Station _____ Date _____

Objective

Upon completion of this job sheet, you will be able to install a cylinder head, cylinder head gasket, and tighten it according to manufacturer's specifications. You must know how to perform these tasks to pass the ASE Engine Repair Test. Before beginning, review **Chapter 10** of AUTOMOTIVE TECHNOLOGY.

These job sheets meet the requirements for **NATEF** task(s): **Cylinder Head and Valve Train Diagnosis and Repair**

Tools and Materials:
AUTOMOTIVE TECHNOLOGY 4e (Thomson, Delmar Learning)
Basic hand tools
Service manual
Torque wrench

NATEF TASKS
I. Engine Repair
Category: B
Task: 2 (P-1)

Protective Gear:
Goggles or safety glasses with side shields

Describe the vehicle being worked on:
Year _____ Make _____ Model _____
VIN _____ Engine type and size _____

PROCEDURE

1. Make sure the sealing surfaces on the engine block and cylinder head are clean. Wipe them down with a clean rag prior to installing the cylinder head.   ☐ Task completed

2. Carefully look over the head bolts. Are they torque-to-yield bolts? What difference does that make during installation?

   _____
   _____

3. Inspect the threads of the bolts and replace any that need to be replaced. Make sure the replacement bolts are an exact duplicate of what was originally used. Your findings:

   _____
   _____

4. Sort the head bolts and identify any that are longer than the others. Are all of your head bolts the same length?

   _____

118 Cylinder Heads and Valves

5. Thoroughly clean the threads of each bolt. Does the service manual recommend that the bolts be put in dry or should they have a lubricant? If yes, what?

   _____

6. If some bolts are longer than others, check the service manual to determine their proper location. Where do the longer head bolts go in this engine?

   _____
   _____

7. Place the cylinder head gasket onto the block and check its fit. Make sure all bores and passages line up properly and that the correct side of the gasket is facing up. ☐ Task completed

8. Carefully lower the cylinder head over the head gasket and onto the block. Were there dowels to help position the head or did you need to guess at the proper position?

   _____
   _____

9. Insert the cylinder head bolts into their proper bore. ☐ Task completed

10. Start each of the bolts by hand-turning them. ☐ Task completed

11. Refer to the service manual for the proper tightening sequence for the head bolts. Describe that sequence here:

    _____
    _____

12. Check the specifications for tightening steps. If the manufacturer recommends steps, describe them here.

    _____
    _____

13. Tighten the bolts according to the service manual's specifications. The final amount of torque on the head bolts should be: _____

Problems Encountered

_____
_____
_____

Instructor's Comments

_____
_____
_____

Cylinder Heads and Valves 119

☐ JOB SHEET / AT 101-24

Valve Timing Check

Name _____ Station _____ Date _____

Objective

Upon completion of this job sheet, you will be able to verify camshaft timing according to manufacturer's specifications. You must know how to perform these tasks to pass the ASE Engine Repair and Engine Performance Tests. Before beginning, review **Chapter 11** of AUTOMOTIVE TECHNOLOGY.

These job sheets meet the requirements for **NATEF** task(s): **Cylinder Head and Valve Train Diagnosis and Repair**

Tools and Materials:
AUTOMOTIVE TECHNOLOGY 4e (Thomson, Delmar Learning)
Spark plug socket
Compression gauge
Remote starter switch
Flashlight
Misc. hand tools
Large breaker bar
New rocker arm or camshaft cover gasket

NATEF TASKS
I. Engine Repair
Category: B
Task: 12 (P-2)
Task: 13 (P-1)

Protective Gear:
Goggles or safety glasses with side shields

Describe the engine being worked on:
Year _____ Make _____ Model _____
VIN _____ Engine type and size _____

PROCEDURE

1. If the timing belt or chain has slipped on the camshaft sprocket, the engine may fail to start because the valves are not properly timed in relation to the crankshaft. When the timing belt or chain has only slipped a few cogs on the camshaft sprocket, the engine has a lack of power, and fuel consumption is excessive. To check valve timing, begin by removing the spark plug from number 1 cylinder. ☐ Task completed

2. Disconnect the positive primary wire from the ignition coil to disable the ignition system. ☐ Task completed

3. Connect a remote control switch to the starter solenoid terminal and the battery terminal on the solenoid. ☐ Task completed

4. Place your thumb on top of the spark plug hole at cylinder #1. If this hole is not accessible, place a compression gauge in the opening. ☐ Task completed

120 Cylinder Heads and Valves

5. Crank the engine until compression is felt at the spark plug hole. Then, slowly crank the engine until the timing mark lines up with the zero-degree position on the timing indicator. The number 1 piston is now at TDC on the compression stroke. On many engines, the timing mark is on the crankshaft pulley, and the timing indicator is mounted above the pulley.   ☐ Task completed

6. Now, slowly crank the engine for one revolution until the timing mark lines up with the zero-degree position on the timing indictor. The number 1 piston is now at TDC on the exhaust stroke.   ☐ Task completed

7. Remove the rocker arm or camshaft cover and install a breaker bar and socket on the crankshaft pulley nut. Observe the valve action while rotating the crankshaft about 30 degrees before and after TDC on the exhaust stroke. In this crankshaft position, the exhaust valve should close a few degrees after TDC on the exhaust stroke, and the intake valve should open a few degrees before TDC on the exhaust stroke. Is this what you observed?   ☐ Task completed

   _____

8. If the valves did not open properly in relation to the crankshaft position, the valve timing is not correct. What should you do to correct it?

   _____

   _____

   _____

   _____

9. If the timing was correct, reinstall the rocker arm or camshaft cover with a new gasket. Tighten the attaching bolts to the proper specification. The recommended torque is _____

10. Reinstall the spark plug and tighten it to the proper specification. The recommended torque is _____

Problems Encountered

_____

_____

_____

Instructor's Comments

_____

_____

_____

Cylinder Heads and Valves   **121**

☐ **JOB SHEET / AT 101-25**

Replace a Timing Belt on an OHC Engine

Name _____ Station _____ Date _____

Objective

Upon completion of this job sheet, you will be able to replace a timing belt on an OHC engine. You must know how to perform these tasks to pass the ASE Engine Repair Test. Before beginning, review **Chapter 10** of AUTOMOTIVE TECHNOLOGY.

These job sheets meet the requirements for **NATEF** task(s): **Cylinder Head and Valve Train Diagnosis and Repair**

Tools and Materials:
AUTOMOTIVE TECHNOLOGY 4e (Thomson, Delmar Learning)
Basic hand tools
Paint stick or chalk
Belt tension gauge

NATEF TASKS
I. Engine Repair
Category: B
Task: 13 (P-1)

Protective Gear:
Goggles or safety glasses with side shields

Describe the engine being worked on:
Year _____ Make _____ Model _____
VIN _____ Engine type and size _____

PROCEDURE

1. Disconnect the negative cable from the battery prior to beginning to remove and replace the timing belt.   ☐ Task completed

2. Carefully remove the timing cover. Be careful not to distort or damage it while pulling it up. With the cover removed, check the immediate area around the belt for wires and other obstacles. If some are found, move them out of the way. What needed to be removed? Did you need to remove other drive belts?

   _____
   _____
   _____

3. Align the timing marks on the camshaft's sprocket with the mark on the cylinder head. If the marks are not obvious, use a paint stick or chalk to clearly mark them.   ☐ Task completed

4. Carefully remove the crankshaft timing sensor and probe holder.   ☐ Task completed

5. Loosen the adjustment bolt on the belt tensioner pulley. It is normally not necessary to remove the tensioner assembly.   ☐ Task completed

122 Cylinder Heads and Valves

6. Slide the belt off the crankshaft sprocket. Be careful not to allow the crankshaft pulley to rotate while doing this. ☐ Task completed

7. To remove the belt from the engine, the crankshaft pulley may need to be removed to slip it off the crankshaft sprocket. Did you need to remove the pulley? What did you need to do to remove the pulley?

   _____
   _____
   _____

8. After the belt has been removed, inspect it for cracks and other damage. Cracks will become more obvious if the belt is twisted slightly. Describe any defects in the belt. **Note:** *Timing belts are always replaced once they have been removed.* When may this not be true?

   _____
   _____
   _____

9. To begin reassembly, place the belt around the crankshaft sprocket. Then reinstall the crankshaft pulley. ☐ Task completed

10. Make sure the timing marks on the crankshaft pulley are lined up with the marks on the engine block. If they are not, carefully rock the crankshaft until the marks are lined up. ☐ Task completed

11. With the timing belt fitted onto the crankshaft sprocket and the crankshaft pulley tightened in place, the crankshaft timing sensor and probe can be reinstalled. ☐ Task completed

12. Align the camshaft sprocket with the timing makers on the cylinder head. Then wrap the timing belt around the camshaft sprocket and allow the belt tensioner to put a slight amount of pressure on the belt. ☐ Task completed

13. Adjust the tension as described in the service manual. Then rotate the engine two complete turns. Recheck the tension. What are the specifications for belt tension? Why do you need to rotate the engine twice before rechecking the tension?

    _____
    _____
    _____
    _____

14. Rotate the engine through two complete turns again, then check the alignment marks on the camshaft and the crankshaft. Any deviation needs to be corrected before the timing cover is reinstalled. ☐ Task completed

Cylinder Heads and Valves

Problems Encountered

Instructor's Comments

☐ JOB SHEET / AT 101-26

Servicing Oil Pressure and Temperature Sensors

Name _____ Station _____ Date _____

Objective

Upon completion of this job sheet, you will be able to inspect, test, and replace oil temperature and pressure switches and sensors. You must know how to perform these tasks to pass the ASE Engine Repair Test. Before beginning, review **Chapters 11 and 20** of AUTOMOTIVE TECHNOLOGY.

These job sheets meet the requirements for **NATEF** task(s): **Cylinder Head and Valve Train Diagnosis and Repair**

Tools and Materials:
AUTOMOTIVE TECHNOLOGY 4e (Thomson, Delmar Learning)
Ohmmeter
Basic hand tools
Oil pressure tester

NATEF TASKS
I. Engine Repair
Category: D
Task: 12 (P-2)

Protective Gear:
Goggles or safety glasses with side shields

Describe the engine being worked on:
Year _____ Make _____ Model _____
VIN _____ Engine type and size _____

PROCEDURE

1. Describe the type(s) of oil gauges and/or warning lights the engine is equipped with.
   _____
   _____
   _____

2. Explain the purpose of each.
   _____
   _____
   _____

3. Locate the specifications for each in the service manual and record the specifications here.
   _____
   _____
   _____

126 Cylinder Heads and Valves

4. When you turn the ignition on with the engine off, do the indicator lamps light? What are the readings on the gauges?

   _____

   _____

   _____

5. Start the engine. Do the lamps turn off? Do the readings on the gauges change?

   _____

   _____

6. What can you conclude so far?

   _____

   _____

   _____

7. With the engine off, carefully examine the area around each of the sensors. Look for signs of oil leakage and record your findings.

   _____

   _____

8. Also look for oil inside the protective boots for the electrical connectors. What can you conclude?

   _____

   _____

9. Disconnect the electrical connector to each of the sensors and connect an ohmmeter from the terminal of the sensor to ground. Compare the reading to the specifications. What can you conclude from this test?

   _____

   _____

10. Start the engine and look at the ohmmeter reading. Compare the reading to the specifications. What can you conclude from this test?

    _____

    _____

11. If the oil pressure sensor is suspected as being bad, note the oil pressure reading shown on the oil pressure gauge on the instrument panel while the engine is idling.

12. Then turn the engine off and remove the sensor. Connect an oil pressure tester to the sensor's bore.   ☐ Task completed

13. Start the engine and allow it to idle. Record the oil pressure shown on the test gauge.

   _____

14. Compare the reading on the test gauge with the reading taken at the instrument panel. What can you conclude?

   _____

   _____

15. Install the sensor or a new one and reconnect the electrical connector to it.   ☐ Task completed

16. If the sensor(s) tested fine but there is still misinformation at the gauges or indicator lamps, the gauge or lamp circuit must be tested. Is it necessary to do so on this vehicle?

   _____

   _____

   _____

   _____

Problems Encountered

_____

_____

_____

Instructor's Comments

_____

_____

_____

SHOP ACTIVITY / AT 101-10

Valve Assemblies

Name _____ Station _____ Date _____

Objective

Upon completion of this activity, you will be able to use various reference materials and instructor notes to identify differences among various manufacturer's valve configurations.

Refer to **Chapter 11** in the AUTOMOTIVE TECHNOLOGY book for additional information.

Tools and Materials:
AUTOMOTIVE TECHNOLOGY 4e (Thomson, Delmar Learning)
All-Data or Mitchell On-Demand
Service manuals
Various automotive engines

Protective Gear:
Safety glasses

PROCEDURE

Using instructor-designated engines and reference materials, describe the components of the valve assembly for five different engines. Identify the differences (for example, some have more than one spring per valve), and explain why these differences exist.

Engine #1:
Year _____ Make _____ Model _____
Engine type and size _____ Reference used _____

1. Number of valves per cylinder? _____
2. Number of valve springs per valve? _____
3. Valve configuration. _____
4. Explain the differences that are found on this engine in comparison with the others.

_____
_____
_____
_____

130   Cylinder Heads and Valves

Engine #2:

Year _____ Make _____ Model _____

Engine type and size _____ Reference used _____

1. Number of valves per cylinder? _____
2. Number of valve springs per valve? _____
3. Valve configuration. _____
4. Explain the differences that are found on this engine in comparison with the others.

_____

_____

_____

_____

_____

Engine #3:

Year _____ Make _____ Model _____

Engine type and size _____ Reference used _____

1. Number of valves per cylinder? _____
2. Number of valve springs per valve? _____
3. Valve configuration. _____
4. Explain the differences that are found on this engine in comparison with the others.

_____

_____

_____

_____

_____

Engine #4:

Year _____ Make _____ Model _____

Engine type and size _____ Reference used _____

1. Number of valves per cylinder? _____
2. Number of valve springs per valve? _____
3. Valve configuration. _____
4. Explain the differences that are found on this engine in comparison with the others.

_____

_____
_____
_____
_____

Engine #5:

Year _____ Make _____ Model _____

Engine type and size _____ Reference used _____

1. Number of valves per cylinder? _____
2. Number of valve springs per valve? _____
3. Valve configuration. _____
4. Explain the differences that are found on this engine in comparison with the others.

_____
_____
_____
_____
_____

Problems Encountered

_____
_____
_____

Instructor's Comments

_____
_____
_____

Instructor's Signature

_____

SHOP ACTIVITY / AT 101-11

Cylinder Heads

Name _____ Station _____ Date _____

Objective

Upon completion of this activity, you will be able to correctly identify the various parts of a cylinder head. Refer to **Chapter 11** in the AUTOMOTIVE TECHNOLOGY book for additional information.

Tools and Materials:
AUTOMOTIVE TECHNOLOGY 4e (Thomson, Delmar Learning)
Cylinder head
OHC Cylinder head

Protective Gear:
Safety glasses

PROCEDURE

Using instructor-designated cylinder heads, identify the various parts and record your findings. Note any irregularities you may see.

A. Camshaft in block cylinder head

_____
_____
_____
_____
_____
_____
_____
_____
_____
_____
_____
_____

134 Cylinder Heads and Valves

B. Overhead camshaft cylinder head

Problems Encountered

Instructor's Comments

Instructor's Signature

CASE STUDY

A customer brings in a 2003 Cavalier with valve noise. List, in proper sequence, the first three checks the technician should make.

1. _____
2. _____
3. _____

INFORMATION SHEET

Engine Sealing and Reassembly

INFORMATION

These job sheets cover the final assembly of the engine assembly. The job sheets cover the proper installation of the major parts of the engine and their associated gaskets. They also cover the proper use of chemicals and sealers during the assembly process. Procedures for starting and breaking in the newly rebuilt engine are also covered.

Careful machining and rebuilding of the engine's parts are necessary for a successful rebuild of an engine. These can be a waste of time if the engine is not assembled properly. Proper reassembly includes the correct tightness of all fasteners and the correct installation of gaskets and sealers. After the parts are installed on the engine, the fasteners should provide a secure mounting and, in many cases, a proper seal.

Most fasteners used to assemble the engine are designed for the specific component they hold in place. Fasteners also have a specific torque specification that must be adhered to. Failure to use the proper fastener or not using the correct torque specifications or tightening sequence can result in premature failure of components and/or leakage.

Engine Sealing and Reassembly 139

☐ JOB SHEET / AT 101-27

Reassemble Engine

Name _____ Station _____ Date _____

Objective

Upon completion of this job sheet, you will be able to reassemble an engine and mount its components using the correct gaskets and sealants. You must know how to perform these tasks to pass the ASE Engine Repair Test. Before beginning, review **Chapter 13** of AUTOMOTIVE TECHNOLOGY.

These job sheets meet the requirements for **NATEF** task(s): **Engine Block Assembly Diagnosis and Repair**

Tools and Materials:

AUTOMOTIVE TECHNOLOGY 4e (Thomson, Delmar Learning)
Straightedge
Flashlight
Feeler gauge
Hydraulic press
Drivers
Block of wood

NATEF TASKS
I. Engine Repair
Category: C
Task: 13 (P-2)
Task: 14 (P-3)
Task: 15 (P-2)

Protective Gear:
Goggles or safety glasses with side shields

Describe the engine being worked on:
Year _____ Make _____ Model _____
VIN _____ Engine type and size _____

PROCEDURE

WARNING: *Make sure every sealant you use on today's engines is oxygen sensor safe.*

1. Visually inspect the bolts. Threads must be clean and undamaged. Discard all bolts that are not acceptable. Describe the condition of the bolts:

   _____
   _____

2. Gather new gaskets for the engine. Never reuse old gaskets. Even if the old gasket appears to be in good condition, it will never seal as well as a new one. Protect the new gaskets by keeping them in their packages until it is time to install them.   ☐ Task completed

3. Make sure all surfaces are free of dirt, oil deposits, rust, old sealer, and gasket material.   ☐ Task completed

4. Check the condition of the balancer shaft or crankshaft pulley hub. Make sure the surface is smooth. If the surface is not smooth, the seal will not be able to seal. What can be done if the pulley hub has a groove in it?

   _____
   _____

140 Engine Sealing and Reassembly

5. Before installing the oil pan and gasket, check the flanges for warpage. Use a straightedge or lay the pan, flange side down, on a flat surface with a flashlight underneath it to spot uneven edges. Carefully check the flange around the bolt holes. What were the results of this check? If the flange is distorted, what should you do?

_____

_____

6. Once it has been determined that the flanges are flat, install the oil pan with a new gasket. ☐ Task completed

7. When replacing the timing cover, remove the old gaskets and seals from the timing cover and engine block. ☐ Task completed

8. Install a new crankshaft seal using a press, seal driver, or hammer and a clean block of wood. When installing the seal, be sure to support the cover underneath to prevent damage. ☐ Task completed

9. If the timing cover extends over the front lip of the oil pan, the front portion of the oil pan gasket will be exposed. With a sharp knife or razor blade, carefully cut off the front exposed portion of the oil pan gasket. Did you need to do this?

_____

10. Apply a light coating of adhesive or sealant on the timing cover and position the gasket on the cover. Finally, mount the timing cover and torque the bolts to specifications. Check the service manual to see what type of adhesive or sealant you should use. Record the manufacturer's recommendations.

_____

_____

11. Install the vibration damper (harmonic balancer) by carefully pounding on it, or using a special installation tool. In most cases, the damper is installed until it bottoms out against the oil slinger and the timing sprocket. It is best to stand the engine block on end and support the crankshaft if the damper must be pounded on. Check the service manual to see how the damper should be installed. Describe the procedure here.

_____

_____

_____

12. Some vibration dampers are held to the crankshaft by a retaining bolt. Be sure to install the large washer behind the retaining bolt on these engines. Tighten this bolt to specifications. The specifications are:

_____

13. Before installing the valve cover, make sure the cover's sealing flange is flat, and then apply contact adhesive to the valve cover's sealing surfaces in small dabs. Mount the valve cover gasket on the valve cover and align it in position. If the gasket has mounting tabs, use them in tandem with the contact adhesive. Allow the adhesive to dry completely before mounting the valve cover on the cylinder head. Torque the mounting bolts to specifications. The specifications are:

   _____

14. The intake manifold gasket seals the joint between the intake manifold and the cylinder head. To be sure the gasket will seal, check its fit before installing it. On steel shim-type gaskets, it is necessary to put a thin and even coat of positioning sealant around the vacuum port openings and a small bead of RTV silicone around the coolant openings. Install the intake manifold with a new gasket and tighten the fastening bolts to the recommended torque specification. The specifications are:

   _____

15. Install the thermostat and water outlet housing. Install the thermostat with the temperature sensor facing into the block. Make sure the gasket is positioned properly. Use the sealant recommended by the manufacturer. Take care not to tighten the housing unevenly. Tighten each mounting bolt a little at a time and tighten to specifications. The specifications are:

   _____

16. Exhaust manifolds may or may not require a gasket; check the service manual. Also check the manual for tightening sequence and torque specifications. Record this information here.

   _____

   _____

17. Place the exhaust manifold into position. Tighten the bolts in the center of the manifold first to prevent cracking it. If there are dowel holes in the exhaust manifold that align with dowels in the cylinder head, make sure that these holes are larger than the dowels. ☐ Task completed

18. Reinstall the engine sling to remove the engine from the engine stand. ☐ Task completed

19. Raise the engine into the air on a suitable hoist, and remove the engine stand mounting head. ☐ Task completed

20. Set the assembled engine on the floor and support it with blocks of wood while attaching the flywheel or flex plate. ☐ Task completed

21. Make sure you use the right flysheel bolts and lock washers. These bolts have very thin heads and the lock washers are thin, Make sure that the bolts are properly torqued and tightened in the correct sequence. The torque specifications are:

   _____

   _____

Problems Encountered

Instructor's Comments

Engine Sealing and Reassembly 143

☐ JOB SHEET / AT 101-28

Adjust Valves on an OHC Engine

Name _____ Station _____ Date _____

Objective

Upon completion of this job sheet, you will have demonstrated the ability to adjust the valves on an OHC engine. You must know how to perform these tasks to pass the ASE Engine Repair Test.

These job sheets meet the requirements for **NATEF** task(s): **Cylinder Head and Valve Train Diagnosis and Repair**

Tools and Materials:

AUTOMOTIVE TECHNOLOGY 4e (Thomson, Delmar Learning)
Hand tools
Feeler gauge
Remote starter button
Allen wrench set
Service manual

NATEF TASKS
I. Engine Repair
Category: B
Task: 11 (P-1)
Task: 16 (P-1)

Protective Gear:

Goggles or safety glasses with side shields

Describe the vehicle being worked on:

Year _____ Make _____ Model _____

VIN _____ Engine type and size _____

Describe what is used to maintain valve lash on the engine:
_____

PROCEDURE

1. Choose the appropriate service manual to determine if the valves are supposed to be adjusted with a cold engine or when the engine is at normal operating temperature. ☐ Task completed

2. Remove necessary hoses and wires to allow the removal of the cam cover (valve cover). ☐ Task completed

3. Adjust the valves according to the procedure described in the service manual for the engine you are working on. ☐ Task completed

4. Re-install the cam cover, and connect any wires or hoses that were disconnected. ☐ Task completed

5. Start the engine to test the operation and inspect for oil leaks. ☐ Task completed

Problems Encountered

Instructor's Comments

Engine Sealing and Reassembly **145**

☐ JOB SHEET / AT 101-29

Apply RTV Silicone Sealant

Name _____ Station _____ Date _____

Objective

Upon completion of this job sheet, you will have demonstrated the ability to properly apply an RTV silicone sealant. You must know how to perform these tasks in order to pass the ASE Engine Repair Test. Before beginning, review the appropriate section under the "Silicone Formed-in-Place Sealants" heading in **Chapter 13** of AUTOMOTIVE TECHNOLOGY.

These job sheets meet the requirements for **NATEF** task(s): **Engine Block Assembly Diagnosis and Repair**

Tools and Materials:
AUTOMOTIVE TECHNOLOGY 4e (Thomson, Delmar Learning)
Dry towel
RTV silicone sealant
Service manual

NATEF TASKS
I. Engine Repair
Category: C
Task: 15 (P-2)

Protective Clothing:
Goggles or safety glasses with side shields

Describe the vehicle being worked on:

Year _____ Make _____ Model _____

VIN _____ Engine type and size _____

Describe the parts being sealed:

_____

PROCEDURE

1. Using the service manual, determine the correct type of RTV sealer to use.   ☐ Task completed

   CAUTION: *The use of the wrong type of sealer may result in failure of the oxygen sensor and/or catalytic converter.*

2. Make sure that the mating surfaces are free of dirt, grease, and oil. Apply a continuous 1/8-in. (3.18 mm) bead on one surface only. Be sure to circle all bolt holes.   ☐ Task completed

   WARNING: *Make sure there is adequate ventilation when applying RTV sealers.*

3. Adjust the shape of the RTV before skin forms (in about 10 minutes). Remove all excess RTV silicone with a dry towel or paper towel.   ☐ Task completed

4. Press the parts together. Do not slide them together.   ☐ Task completed

5. Tighten all retaining bolts to the manufacturer's specified torque.   ☐ Task completed

Problems Encountered

Instructor's Comments

Engine Sealing and Reassembly   147

☐ JOB SHEET / AT 101-30

Prime an Engine's Lubrication System

Name _____ Station _____ Date _____

Objective

Upon completion of this job sheet, you will be able to prime an engine's lubrication system after the engine has been rebuilt. You must know how to perform these tasks to pass the ASE Engine Repair Test. Before beginning, review **Chapter 13** of AUTOMOTIVE TECHNOLOGY.

These job sheets meet the requirements for **NATEF** task(s): **Lubrication and Cooling System Diagnosis and Repair**

Tools and Materials:
AUTOMOTIVE TECHNOLOGY 4e (Thomson, Delmar Learning)
Reversible electric drill
Priming tool
Basic hand tools

NATEF TASKS
I. Engine Repair
Category: D
Task: 1 (P-1)
Task: 2 (P-2)

Protective Gear:
Goggles or safety glasses with side shields

Describe the vehicle being worked on:
Year _____ Make _____ Model _____
VIN _____ Engine type and size _____

PROCEDURE

NOTE: *After an engine has been rebuilt, it must be pre-oiled to prevent damage to engine parts when it is first started. This job sheet gives the procedure for manual pre-oiling. Fill out the part of the job sheet that matches the equipment and engine you are working with. Also make sure you follow the guidelines given in the service manual.*

Manual Pre-Oiling

1. Make sure the engine has the proper amount of oil and the right type. Then, remove the distributor. ☐ Task completed

2. If you have a priming tool to drive the oil pump drive shaft, move to the next step. If you do not, select a socket that fits positively on the oil pump drive shaft located in the distributor shaft bore in the engine block. What size socket will you use?

   _____

3. Affix the priming tool or socket with an extension to the electric drill ☐ Task completed

4. Refer to the service manual and determine what direction the distributor normally rotates in. Is it clockwise or counterclockwise?

   _____

5. Set the drill to rotate in that direction. ☐ Task completed

6. Fit the priming tool or socket onto the oil pump drive. ☐ Task completed

148 Engine Sealing and Reassembly

7. Spin the drive until a resistance to turning is felt. What does this indicate?

   _____

8. Continue to spin for an additional 30 seconds. ☐ Task completed

9. Stop spinning the drive and rotate the crankshaft 90 degrees and repeat the process. ☐ Task completed

10. Again stop spinning the drive and rotate the crankshaft 90 degrees and repeat the process. ☐ Task completed

11. And one last time, stop spinning the drive and rotate the crankshaft 90 degrees and repeat the process. Why is it necessary to rotate the crankshaft?

    _____

    _____

12. Reinstall the distributor, making sure it is positioned properly. ☐ Task completed

Alternative Manual Pre-Oiling

1. Make sure the oil filter is filled with clean, fresh oil before installing it. Also make sure the engine has the proper amount of oil and the right type. ☐ Task completed

2. Connect the battery terminals and disable the ignition. ☐ Task completed

3. Crank the engine with the starter for 30 seconds, then stop. ☐ Task completed

4. Wait at least 30 seconds, then crank the engine again or 30 seconds, then stop. Why do you need to stop after cranking for 30 seconds?

   _____

5. Repeat the process above as many times as necessary. The goal is to have an oil pressure reading on the oil pressure gauge or to have the oil warning light turn off. How many times did you need to repeat this process?

   _____

6. reconnect the ignition system and start the engine. Check the oil pressure at idle. What was the pressure? Does it match specifications?

   _____

   _____

Problems Encountered

_____

_____

Instructor's Comments

_____

_____

Engine Sealing and Reassembly

SHOP ACTIVITY / AT 101-12

Torque Specifications

Name _____ Station _____ Date _____

Objective

Upon completion of this activity, you will be able to find and record the torque specification values for instructor-designated engine-components.

Refer to **Chapter 4** in the AUTOMOTIVE TECHNOLOGY book for additional information.

Tools and Materials:
AUTOMOTIVE TECHNOLOGY 4e (Thomson, Delmar Learning)
Service manuals
All-Data®

Protective Gear:
Text

Describe the engine being worked on:
Year _____ Make _____ Model _____
VIN _____ Engine type and size _____

PROCEDURE

Record the torque specifications and procedures for the following components.

1. Cylinder head bolts   _____
2. Intake manifold   _____
3. Oil pan   _____
4. Valve/cam covers   _____
5. Water pump bolts   _____
6. Exhaust manifold   _____
7. Timing cover bolts   _____

Problems Encountered

_____
_____
_____

Instructor's Comments

_____

_____

_____

Instructor's Signature

_____

SHOP ACTIVITY / AT 101-13

Engine Sealing

Name _____ Station _____ Date _____

Objective

Upon completion of this activity, you will be able to describe various automotive sealing materials and their functions.

Refer to **Chapter 13** in the AUTOMOTIVE TECHNOLOGY book for additional information.

Tools and Materials:
AUTOMOTIVE TECHNOLOGY 4e (Thomson, Delmar Learning)
Service manuals
All-Data® or Mitchell On-Demand®
Instructor notes

Protective Gear:
N/A

PROCEDURE

Describe what each of the following gaskets must do or seal. Include in your description everything that is sealed by the gasket.

1. Cylinder head gasket

   _____
   _____
   _____
   _____

2. Intake manifold gasket

   _____
   _____
   _____
   _____

3. Water pump gasket _____

   _____
   _____
   _____

4. Oil pan gasket

5. Valve cover gasket

Problems Encountered

Instructor's Comments

Instructor's Signature